KU-637-830

Contents

Access to History

General Editor: Keith Randell

The Origins of the American Civil War 1846-61

Alan Farmer

Hodder & Stoughton

A MEMBER OF THE HODDER HEADLINE GROUP

The cover illustration is a portrait of John Brown (Courtesy of Range Pictures Ltd)

Some other titles in the series:

The American Civil War 1861-65   ISBN 0 340 65870 3
Alan Farmer

The Reconstruction and Effects of the American   ISBN 0 340 67935 2
Civil War 1865-77
Alan Farmer

The USA and the Cold War 1945-63   ISBN 0 340 67963 8
Oliver Edwards

Prosperity, Depression and the New Deal   ISBN 0 340 65871 X
Peter Clements

Order queries: Please contact Bookpoint Ltd, 39 Milton Park, Abingdon,
Oxon OX14 4TD. Telephone: (44) 01235 400414. Fax: (44) 01235 400454.
Lines are open from 9 am - 6 pm Monday to Saturday, with a 24-hour
message answering service. Email address: orders@bookpoint.co.uk

British Library Cataloguing in Publication Data

Farmer, Alan, 1948–
    The Origins of the American Civil War. – (Access to
    history)
    1. Slavery – United States – History 2. United States –
    History – Civil War, 1861-1865. 3. United States –
    Civil War, 1861-1865 – Causes
    I. Title
    973.7'11

ISBN 0–340–65869–X

First published 1996

Impression number   12 11 10 9 8 7 6 5
Year   2004 2003 2002 2001 2000

Copyright © 1996 Alan Farmer

Typeset by Sempringham Publishing Services, Bedford.
Printed in Great Britain for Hodder & Stoughton Educational,
a division of Hodder Headline Plc, 338, Euston Road, London NW1 3BH
by Redwood Books, Trowbridge, Wiltshire.

Preface

To the general reader

Although the *Access to History* series has been designed with the needs of students studying the subject at higher examination levels very much in mind, it also has a great deal to offer the general reader. The main body of the text (i.e. ignoring the Study Guides at the ends of chapters) forms a readable and yet stimulating survey of a coherent topic as studied by historians. However, each author's aim has not merely been to provide a clear explanation of what happened in the past (to interest and inform): it has also been assumed that most readers wish to be stimulated into thinking further about the topic and to form opinions of their own about the significance of the events that are described and discussed (to be challenged). Thus, although no prior knowledge of the topic is expected on the reader's part, she or he is treated as an intelligent and thinking person throughout. The author tends to share ideas and possibilities with the reader, rather than passing on numbers of so-called 'historical truths'.

To the student reader

There are many ways in which the series can be used by students studying History at a higher level. It will, therefore, be worthwhile thinking about your own study strategy before you start your work on this book. Obviously, your strategy will vary depending on the aim you have in mind, and the time for study that is available to you.

If, for example, you want to acquire a general overview of the topic in the shortest possible time, the following approach will probably be the most effective:

1 Read Chapter 1 and think about its contents.
2 Read the 'Making notes' section at the end of Chapter 2 and decide whether it is necessary for you to read this chapter.
3 If it is, read the chapter, stopping at each heading to note down the main points that have been made.
4 Repeat stage 2 (and stage 3 where appropriate) for all the other chapters.

If, however, your aim is to gain a thorough grasp of the topic, taking however much time is necessary to do so, you may benefit from carrying out the same procedure with each chapter, as follows:

1 Read the chapter as fast as you can, and preferably at one sitting.
2 Study the flow diagram at the end of the chapter, ensuring that you understand the general 'shape' of what you have just read.

3 Read the 'Making notes' section (and the 'Answering essay questions' section, if there is one) and decide what further work you need to do on the chapter. In particularly important sections of the book, this will involve reading the chapter a second time and stopping at each heading to think about (and to write a summary of) what you have just read.

4 Attempt the 'Source-based questions' section. It will sometimes be sufficient to think through your answers, but additional understanding will often be gained by forcing yourself to write them down.

When you have finished the main chapters of the book, study the 'Further Reading' section and decide what additional reading (if any) you will do on the topic.

This book has been designed to help make your studies both enjoyable and successful. If you can think of ways in which this could have been done more effectively, please write to tell me. In the meantime, I hope that you will gain greatly from your study of History.

Keith Randell

Acknowledgements

Cover - a portrait of John Brown, courtesy of Range Pictures Ltd. Chicago Historical Society, p 42.

The publishers would like to thank the following for permission to reproduce material in the volume:

Simon and Schuster for extracts from *The Encyclopaedia of the Confederacy*; Touchstone for extracts fron *The Causes of the American Civil War*, Kenneth Stampp (ed); Harper & Row for extracts from *The American People: Creating a Nation and Society*, Gary B. Nash (Ed *et al*); Penguin for *The Portable Abraham Lincoln*, Andrew Dalbanco (Ed); HarperCollins for an extract from *The Lincoln-Douglas Debates*, Harold Holzer (Ed).

Every effort has been made to trace and acknowledge ownership of copyright. The Publishers will be glad to make suitable arrangements with any copyright holders whom it has not been possible to contact.

CHAPTER 1

Introduction: The Origins of the American Civil War

1 'The Great Experiment'

Prior to 1861 the history of the USA had been in many ways a remarkable success story. The small, predominantly English settlements of the early seventeenth century had expanded rapidly, so much so that by the end of the eighteenth century they had been able to win independence from Britain. The United States, which in 1776 had only controlled a narrow strip of land along the Atlantic seaboard, continued to expand westwards. In the late eighteenth century, settlers crossed the Appalachian Mountains into Tennessee, Kentucky, and the territory south of the Great Lakes. In 1802-3 the USA doubled in size when it purchased the Louisiana territory from France. By 1850, largely as a result of the annexation of Texas (1845) and gains made after success in the Mexican War (1846-8), the United States extended from the Atlantic to the Pacific. By 1860 the original 13 states had increased to 33. Many Americans thought it was their 'manifest destiny' to take over the whole of North and Central America.

The country had also had considerable economic, social and political success. By 1860 white Americans enjoyed a better standard of living than any other people on earth. The United States' political system, republican, federal and democratic - was the pride of most Americans and the envy of most British and European radicals. By the mid-nineteenth century, the American people were probably the most equal and certainly the best educated in the world. Not surprisingly, many Americans considered themselves to be the world's most civilised and fortunate people: in novelist Henry Melville's view, 'The peculiar chosen people, the Israel of our time'.

It should be said that not everyone benefited from what many Americans saw as the 'great experiment'. During the 250 years that had elapsed since the coming of the first English settlers, Native Americans had lost most of their land. By 1860 only the Plains Indians still clung precariously to territory west of the Mississippi river. The other major ethnic group that might have questioned the notion of a great experiment were the African Americans, whose ancestors had been transported to America as slaves. Although the United States had declared the slave trade illegal in 1808, slavery continued in the American South. In 1860 there were some four million slaves. This was a great anomaly in a country proud of the 1776 Declaration of Independence which stated categorically that 'we hold these truths to be self-evident; that all men are created equal'! In the opinion of many Northerners in 1860, the fact that slavery - the 'peculiar institution' -

still existed was the major failing of the great experiment.

If slavery was the major failing of the great experiment pre-1861, the Civil War (1861-5) remains, without doubt, the greatest failure in American history. It represented an utter breakdown of the normal political processes. Political passions split the Union and as a result some 620,000 Americans were to die in the bloodiest war fought in the Western world between 1815 and 1914. The blood-letting was similar (proportionally) to that in Europe in the First World War. More Americans died in the Civil War than in all America's subsequent wars (to date) put together. 'The fiery trial' was the USA's greatest test threatening the continuation of the great experiment.

2 What to Call the War?

Since 1861 historians - and politicians - have argued over a name for the conflict. By far the most popular name today is the 'Civil War'. Both sides used this term throughout the four year struggle. The conflict was indeed a civil war in states like Missouri and Kentucky where brother sometimes did fight brother. However, this was not the norm. In reality, the war was waged by two separate geographical regions: most Northerners were on the Union side and most Southerners were on the Confederate side. Civil War, therefore, is not a totally satisfactory title. Moreover, the term implies that two different groups were fighting for control of a single government when in actual fact the Confederacy was seeking to exist independently. After 1865 Southerners frequently called the conflict 'The War Between the States', a term popularised by Alexander Stephens, the Confederate Vice President. But this title is rather cumbersome and not quite correct: the contest was waged not by states but by two organised governments - the Union and the Confederacy. Northerners have sometimes referred to the conflict as 'The War of the Rebellion' - another cumbersome term. Moreover, the struggle was more than a rebellion: it lasted four years and was fought by two governments respecting the rules of war. Other terms which have occasionally been used to describe the conflict (each of which has a connotation that offers a different explanation of what the struggle was about) include 'The War for Southern Independence', 'The Confederate War', 'The War for Secession', 'The War against Slavery', and 'The War for Nationality'. It should be said that virtually everyone now calls the war the Civil War. This book will be no exception!

3 North versus South

By withdrawing from the United States in 1860-1, the Southern states were in effect embarking on a course of nation-making, which happened in much of Europe in the nineteenth century. Southerners came to believe that the South possessed a character quite distinct from that of the North - distinct enough to qualify their region (or section) for separate nationhood. They looked upon themselves as constituting a suppressed nationality, comparable to the Italians or the Poles.

However, many historians believe that the Civil War had more to do with the development of Southern nationalism than Southern nationalism had to do with bringing about Civil War. It could be argued that there was far more uniting than dividing North and South in 1861. Northerners and Southerners spoke the same language. They had the same religion. They shared the same legal system, political culture and pride in their common heritage. Most also held similar - racist - views, accepting without question that African Americans were inferior to whites. Common economic interest seemed to bind the two sections together. 'In brief and in short', said Senator Thomas Hart Benson, 'the two halves of the Union were made for each other, as much as Adam and Eve'.

In the mid-twentieth century some historians were convinced that, given these similarities, Civil War was far from 'irrepressible' or inevitable. 'Revisionist' historians claimed that a small minority of Yankee zealots and Southern 'fire-eaters' were responsible for raising tensions in the years before 1861. The revisionists blamed blundering politicians for failing to find a compromise solution to the 'impending crisis'.

However, most historians today absolve the blundering generation of politicians. They stress that Northerners and Southerners were deeply divided. In particular, they held irreconcilable views about slavery - especially the desirability of slavery expansion. In consequence, Civil War was - to a large extent - 'irrepressible'. This modern view of the origins of the Civil War would probably have been accepted by President Abraham Lincoln. In March 1865, a few weeks before his assassination, he expressed the opinion that slavery was 'somehow' responsible for the start of the war. This book will not dissent from that view. Slavery was crucial. It was the issue which led Southerners to secede from the Union in 1860-1. The main concern of this book is to explain not whether but rather how and why slavery brought about the Civil War.

4 Southern Blame

Throughout the Civil War and for many years afterwards, Northerners blamed Southerners for the war and Southerners blamed Northerners. In the mid-twentieth century 'revisionist' historians were quite happy to mete out blame - and were reasonably even handed in so doing - castigating fanatics and bigots in both sections. On balance, though, the revisionists tended to focus most of their criticism on Northern abolitionists who attacked the 'peculiar institution' and the South as a whole - thus goading Southerners into a defensive response. More recently historians have largely eschewed the notion of 'blame', preferring instead simply to explain how and why the Civil War occurred. It is impossible, however, for historians to take a totally objective stance and to avoid judgement. With the advantage of hindsight, historians are in a position to judge the actions both of individuals and whole societies in the past. With that hindsight it seems obvious that Southern politicians did blunder into war in 1861. However, it would be wrong simply to condemn Southern politicians. For the most part, the politicians represented the views of their constituents: most Southerners were swept by an irrational tide of emotion after Lincoln's election success in November 1860. As a result, Southerners embarked on a course of action that was always likely to lead to war - and a war that they were always likely to lose. It is easy for historians to see this. But the likely results of secession and war were apparent to many Southerners - and most Northerners - in 1861. It is thus fair to point the finger of blame at the South.

There are many similarities between the actions of the South in 1861 and the actions of Japan in 1941. Both the Southerners and the Japanese felt that they had been pushed into a corner from which there was no honourable escape. Honour replaced reason. Dreams replaced reality. Both the Confederate states and Japan closed their eyes to the likely outcome of their actions. Both actually fired the first shots of the war - the Confederates at Fort Sumter in April 1861; the Japanese at Pearl Harbour in December 1941. By so doing they succeeded in provoking conflict and uniting against them the whole of the USA in 1941 and what remained of the United States in 1861. Winston Churchill commented in December 1941 that the Japanese, by attacking Britain and the USA, had embarked on 'a very considerable undertaking'. The same could be said of the South's decision to go to war with the North in 1861.

As a result of a series of Southern blunders, one in four white male Southerners of military age died: the South's profitable economy was devastated; and slavery - the institution which the South had gone to war to defend and which was not under any immediate threat in 1860-1 - ended. Why the South acted as impulsively and irrationally as it did is the central issue of this book.

Working on *'Introduction: The Origins of the American Civil War'*

This chapter has two main objectives: to give you a (very basic) background of the United States' position in the mid-nineteenth century; and to provide you with an overview of some of the debates about the causes of the war. You do not need to make detailed notes. But as you read the rest of the book, watch out for some of the issues raised in this chapter and try to reach your own judgement. Was the war 'repressible' or 'irrepressible'? How important was slavery in bringing about war? Were Southerners really to blame for the war?

CHAPTER 2

The USA in the Mid-nineteenth Century

1 Introduction

By the mid-nineteenth century, most Americans were proud of the achievements of their country and optimistic about its future. There seemed good cause for this optimism. Ante-bellum (pre-war) America was one of the world's most prosperous and enterprising countries. Charles Dickens remarked that while the watchword of Britain was 'All right' that of America was 'Go ahead'. A belief in irreversible progress, including material betterment, captivated most Americans by the mid-nineteenth century. But there was a threatening cloud on the horizon. This was the fact that Northern and Southern states were growing more apart, economically, socially, culturally and politically. The main reason for this division was slavery.

2 The American Political System

The American political system rested on the Constitution drawn up in 1787. The Constitution's 'Founding Fathers' had established a federal system, whereby power would be divided between the central (or federal) government in Washington and the individual states. The Founding Fathers, accepting that sovereignty should be founded on the people, set out to create a system of checks and balances that would prevent any branch of government being in a position to tyrannise the people or any group of people being able to ride rough shod over the rights of others.

The federal government had an executive branch headed by the President; a legislative branch - Congress, compromising the Senate and the House of Representatives; and a judiciary, headed by the Supreme Court.

As well as the federal government in Washington, each state also has its own government. Interestingly, by 1850 the majority of the 30 states then in the Union owed their existence to a creative act of the federal government. In the late eighteenth century the USA had devised a system for admitting new states. New areas first assumed territorial status, electing and establishing a territorial government - under the federal government. Once the population of a territory had reached 60,000 it could submit its proposed constitution (invariably cribbed from other states) to Congress and apply to become a state. If the application was approved, the territory became a fully-fledged state.

Most Americans prided themselves on their form of government - and with good cause. By the mid-nineteenth century the United States had the most democratic system of government on earth. By the 1820s most white males had the right to vote and hold office. The rise of democracy is often associated with President Andrew Jackson (1829-37). Jackson benefitted from - rather than created - the democratic tide. There were limits to that tide. Women and most African Americans were not allowed to participate in the electoral process.

Nevertheless, mid-nineteenth century America was far more democratic than Britain where relatively few men could vote. In the 1830s and 1840s a group of reformers known as the Chartists demanded radical changes to the British electoral system. Most of the Chartist demands already operated in the USA. In most American states there were no property qualifications for office-holders; Congressmen were paid a salary; there was near universal white manhood suffrage; federal and state elections were not annual - but they were at least biennial; there was a move to equal electoral districts; and ballots were used virtually everywhere.

Thus the ordinary American white male voter had potentially great political power. Indeed, candidates for public office often found it expedient not only to extol the common man but also to claim kinship with him: it was thought to be a political advantage to have been born in a log cabin or to have risen from 'rags to riches'. An American political vocabulary developed which drew heavily upon images familiar to the common man. An obscure candidate for office was a 'dark horse': a defeated incumbent was a 'lame duck': politicians made 'stump speeches', 'sat on the fence' and put 'planks' together to make a 'platform'; a sweeping electoral victory was a 'landslide'. So democratic was the USA that by the 1850s judges were elected in most of the states. 'Everybody', wrote one Indiana pioneer, 'expected at some time to be a candidate for something; or that his uncle would be; or his cousin, or his cousin's wife's cousin's friend would be'.

The following extract, written in 1850, gives an impression of democracy in action at local level:

1 The President has one postmaster in every village: but the inhabitants of that village choose their own selectmen, their own assessors of taxes, their own school-committee, their own overseers of the poor, their own surveyors of highways, and the
5 incumbents of half a dozen other little offices corresponding to those which, in bureaucratic governments, are filled by appointment of the sovereign. In all these posts, which are really important public trusts, the villagers are trained to the management of affairs, and acquire a comprehensiveness of view, a practical administra-
10 tive talent, and a knowledge of business ... This training is very general; for owing to our republican liking for rotation in office, the incumbents of these humble posts are changed every year or two.

By the mid-nineteenth century the USA had two main political parties - the Democrats and the Whigs. These parties operated at every level of politics - in local, state, national and presidential elections. The so-called second party system, at its height from 1840 to 1852, had begun to develop in the 1820s but did not fully crystallise until the late 1830s. President Andrew Jackson was very much the catalyst behind this development. Many Americans loved him. Others hated him. His supporters became known as the Democrats. His opponents eventually called themselves Whigs. The two parties, although operating nationally, were not as united as modern political parties. They were really an assortment of state parties which only came together every four years to nominate a presidential candidate, devise a national platform and try to co-ordinate campaign activities. The fact that Presidents could appoint large numbers of officials was crucial. To the victors went the spoils. Those who worked for the successful party were often rewarded with office or government contracts.

However, presidential elections were four years apart. In the gap Whig and Democrat parties at state level went their separate ways, interpreting national party principles in a manner best suited to their local constituencies. It is thus difficult to generalise about the two parties. It is sometimes claimed that there were few differences between the parties and that they were essentially Tweedledum and Tweedledee, at best simply representing different ethnic, sectional and religious groups. But others claim that the party coalitions had very different political and economic ideologies which attracted - or appalled - voters of the various groups. There are elements of truth in both sets of views.

The Democrats based their ideology on that of Andrew Jackson. A self-made man, who had risen - by luck and talent - to become a successful soldier, politician and wealthy Southern landowner, Jackson had claimed to represent the common man against the interests of privilege. (Democrat leaders, like Jackson himself, were often far from 'common' - or poor.) Jackson, while being an activist President, had supported state rights and opposed federal intervention in most aspects of American life. He was also highly suspicious of 'monied' interests. Democrat views, especially on economic matters, were solidified as a result of the economic 'Panic of 1837' and the subsequent depression that gripped the USA until the early 1840s. The Democrats, in power when the depression began, blamed it on banks and too much paper money. They condemned government intervention in economic matters and held the view that the economy would ultimately right itself, especially if tariffs were lowered and the USA was able to expand westwards. They believed the best way to protect liberty, and thereby advance the general welfare, was for the state to do nothing. In the Democrat view, most issues (not least slavery) should be left to individual states to decide and should not be determined by Congress. The Democrats were strongest in the South and West. But the party could also usually count on the support of many working-class voters in the Northern cities - not least from Irish Catholics.

The Whigs had grown up as an amorphous group who had relatively little in common except their opposition to Andrew Jackson. As a result, they are sometimes seen as an unprincipled coalition, held together by nothing other than common antipathy towards the Democrats. By the early 1840s, however, the Whigs had developed a reasonably consistent ideology. Most favoured stronger federal government and positive government intervention (at every level) in economic and social matters. Whigs usually supported the recreation of a national bank, higher tariffs, and federal and state support for internal improvements, especially for railway building and river development. Having faith in the state as an agent of change, Whigs stood for 'improvement' generally. Northern Whigs, in particular, often favoured the creation of public (i.e. state) school systems, supported 'good' causes like temperance reform, and were more likely to be anti-slavery than Democrats. Many were also suspicious of Catholic immigrants. Whig support tended to be strongest in the North, especially in New England. But the Whigs often did well in a number of Southern and Western states, especially North Carolina and Kentucky. Most Whigs were native-born Americans. The Whigs and Democrats really were Tweedledum and Tweedledee, it is difficult to explain the interest aroused by politics in election after election (at every level) and the high voter turn-outs. Political campaigns generated real excitement. Both parties held open-air debates, barbecues, torchlight processions, and distributed a massive amount of campaign literature. Party-subsidised newspapers helped shape political sentiment and raised tensions by regularly indulging in scurrilous attacks on the political enemy.

Throughout the 1840s most Americans committed themselves to one of the two parties and remained remarkably loyal to their 'side'. Changing one's party was a difficult and uncomfortable decision - so much so that voters usually either voted for their party or abstained. In many respects political allegiances were similar to present-day football allegiances. Indeed politics was probably the most popular spectator and participant 'sport' of the day: party activities offered excitement, entertainment and camaraderie. The political game was highly competitive and Whig and Democrat supporters looked forward to defeating the enemy. Political rallies drew remarkably large attendances (of men and women) and 'fans' often dressed for the occasion wearing the regalia of their party. Oddly, the main 'stars' - the presidential candidates - rarely participated much in the campaigns. Instead they retreated to their homes (usually a mansion rather than a log cabin), adopted the role of the 'Mute Tribune', and let their supporters do the dirty work for them. But presidential campaigns were by no means the only political 'events'. Elections were far more frequent at state and local level. Different states held elections in different months and in different years. In virtually every month of every year, Congressmen, state governors or state legislatures were elected somewhere in the USA.

The Democrat party was usually the dominant party. Between 1840 and 1854 it held a majority of seats in both the House of Representatives and the Senate in five of the seven Congresses. Many Whig leaders believed the only way to win the presidency was to nominate popular military heroes as candidates and fight 'hurrah' campaigns in which the party made plenty of noise but said little about issues or policy. However, Whig existence and success also depended upon the party's ability to provide a genuine alternative to the Democrats at all levels of politics. Most voters reacted in a rational way to what state and national governments did. Given that state governments more actively involved themselves in people's lives than the federal government, how well parties were perceived to perform at state level was often crucial in determining how people voted.

Although the Democrats were usually the more popular party, most national elections were remarkably close. The 1844 presidential election is a good example. James Polk was the Democrat candidate. The Whigs nominated Henry Clay. The Liberty Party, a small anti-slavery party, put forward James Birney. Polk defeated Clay by 170 to 105 votes in the electoral college. But in terms of the popular vote he won by only 38,000 votes out of the 2,600,000 cast. A shift of 6,000 voters in New York state (which had over 30 electoral college votes) would have given Clay both the state and the presidency. Although Birney won only 62,300 votes (2.3 per cent), his standing probably decided the election. Many of those who voted for Birney in New York would otherwise have voted for Clay. Clay would then have become President.

Despite the fierce inter-party rivalry, government in the USA had a limited impact on the lives of most Americans. The checks and balances system ensured that there was every likelihood that one political group would control the presidency or the Senate but not the House of Representatives or the Supreme Court. This meant it was difficult for the federal government actually to do very much. The fact that many matters were seen as state and not federal concerns was another limiting factor. So too was the notion - strongly held by the Democrats - that it was not government's responsibility to intervene much in social and economic matters. (Even Whigs accepted there was a limit to what governments could do.)

The federal government in Washington comprised only a handful of departments - the State Department (which had a staff of just 18 in 1850), the Treasury Department, the Interior Department, the Post Office, the Navy Department, and the War Department. In 1860 there were 36,672 people on the federal government pay roll (excluding the armed forces). No less than 30,269 of these were employed by the Post Office.

The actions of state legislatures impinged more on most Americans' day-to-day lives than the actions of the federal government. Apart from the postmaster, ordinary Americans rarely came across a federal official. They did not even pay direct taxes to Washington. Instead they paid taxes to their state which then paid Washington the state's due. Individual states were responsible for matters like education, looking after the poor, maintaining public health, banking, railway building, voting, and slavery. This is not to say that state governments impinged much on ordinary Americans' daily lives. Government of any kind was hardly significant and Americans were among the most lightly taxed people anywhere in the world. Most Americans, quite naturally, approved of this state of affairs.

3 'A Society of Equals'?

In the 1830s a perceptive Frenchman, Alexander De Tocqueville, visited the USA. Afterwards he wrote a book recounting his experiences. What struck him most was the fact that America seemed a far more equal society than that he was used to in Europe. De Tocqueville labelled America, 'a society of equals'. He noted there was no 'feudal' hierarchy - no sovereign, no court, no established aristocracy or church leaders. Instead there was a real opportunity for men of talent and ambition to rise to the top. Many historians today are suspicious of this (early) notion of the 'American dream'. Black slaves, Native Americans, and women were far from equal in nineteenth century America. Moreover, there were great inequalities of wealth among white males and those inequalities were increasing. In 1860 the top 5 per cent of free adult males owned 53 per cent of the wealth. The bottom 50 per cent owned only 1 per cent. Family standing and inherited wealth were vital assets in terms of individual advancement in mid-nineteenth century America as in most European societies.

Nevertheless, De Tocqueville's claim did have some basis. Compared with Europe, there was rapid social mobility in the USA and opportunities for those with luck and ability. Men like Vanderbilt (who made his fortune in transport) and McCormick (associated with farm machinery) rose from 'rags to riches'. So too did Rockefeller, Mark Twain, Abraham Lincoln - and thousands more Americans. The American dream attracted millions of immigrants to the USA in the mid-nineteenth century. By no means all prospered. But enough did so to keep the dream alive. The dream - and the reality - of social mobility may have helped mitigate class consciousness and conflict in the USA.

Women's status in mid-nineteenth century American society has been a subject of considerable recent debate. There was far less debate at the time. The mid-nineteenth century assigned distinctly unequal roles to men and women. Women were seen - and most saw themselves - essentially as home-makers. Only 25 per cent of white women worked outside the home pre-marriage and fewer than 5 per cent did so while they were married. In most cases marriage was for life. The notion that women's place was in the home was disseminated by both the Church and the growing publishing industry. Today, historians debate the extent to which the 'cult of domesticity' was a setback for women. Many would claim it was. After all, most nineteenth century American men tended to see women as subordinates whose place was in the kitchen, looking after the children, at Church or in bed. Women were denied the same social and political rights as men. They could not vote. In many states wives could not even own property. But some historians have argued that the 'cult of domesticity' actually gave women some power, if only because they usually 'controlled' their families. They had responsibility for the children. (By 1850 the average white woman had 5 children, compared with 7 in 1800.) Often seen as the guardians of morality, women tended to set family values and were greater church-goers than men. Middle-class women played a leading role in many of the reform movements that were a feature of mid-nineteenth century American life, especially abolitionism and temperance. Interestingly, there was a considerable improvement in women's education in the USA. By 1850 most were as well educated as men. An increasing number of women were becoming teachers.

While the national mood seemed at best indifferent and at worst hostile to extending women's social and political rights, thanks to great efforts by a small number of - mainly upper class - feminists like Lucretia Mott and Elizabeth Stanton, there was some move in the direction of women's rights. A feminist convention meeting at Seneca Falls in July 1848 declared that 'All men and women are created equal', demanded that women should have the right to vote, and pressed for equality in education, marriage, property holding and employment. By 1860 about half the states had passed laws recognising married women's property rights. But that was the limit of the feminists' success.

4 'People of Plenty'

The historian David Potter (accurately) described the Americans of the mid-nineteenth century as the 'People of Plenty'. Prosperity and growth seem to be the two words which best describe America's economic development in the first half of the nineteenth century. The country, with its enormous reserves of almost every commodity - fertile land, timber, minerals - and its network of navigable rivers, almost begged to be developed. Not everybody got rich but almost everybody aspired to do so, and many succeeded. From 1800 to 1850 the United States' gross national product increased seven fold and per capita income doubled. The United States' population grew massively, doubling every 25 years or so. In 1840 it stood at 17,000,000; by 1860 it had reached 31,000,000. This was the result of both natural increase and immigration. In the 1840s and 1850s hundreds of thousands of

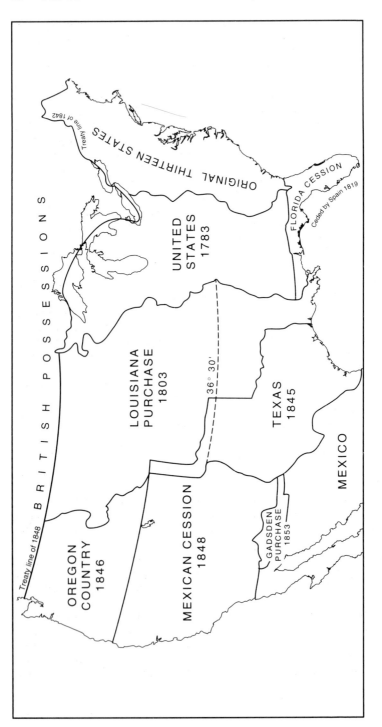

Growth of the United States 1776-1854

Europeans, especially Irish and Germans, poured across the Atlantic. By 1860 immigrants made up almost half the population in some of America's main cities.

The population was young: in 1850 52 per cent of all American whites were under 20. It was also mobile. Some Americans moved to find work in the growing towns. Others moved westwards to settle on the largely unpopulated prairies. In the early nineteenth century Americans had in-filled the area between the Appalachian Mountains and the Mississippi river. Between 1815 and 1850 the population west of the Appalachians grew three times as fast as the population of the original 13 states. By 1850 one in two Americans lived west of the Appalachians. Many moved west - and west again. Abraham Lincoln's family was typical. Abraham's father was born in Virginia in 1778: in 1782 he was taken to Kentucky where Abraham was born in 1809. In 1816 the Lincoln family moved to Indiana. In 1831 Abraham Lincoln moved further west to Illinois. Most people tended to migrate due west into immediate adjacent land: Northerners settled the North-west: Southerners the South-west.

In 1840 the Mississippi was still the effective western frontier of the United States. The dry, treeless area beyond the river was referred to as the 'great desert' in atlases. However, from the 1840s an increasing number of Americans began crossing the great plains and the Rocky Mountains to settle on the Pacific coast. Most Americans thought it was their 'manifest destiny' - their God-given right and race mission - to take over the whole North American continent and spread civilisation. The westward expansion occurred at the expense of Native Americans and Mexicans. Few whites considered even 'civilised' Indians equal to whites. By 1860 Indian lands west of the Mississippi were no longer safe. White settlers were looking for new lands to develop. Already by 1860 some 4,000,000 Americans lived west of the Mississippi.

The USA was still essentially an agricultural country. In 1860 only one in five Americans lived in a 'town' (defined as a settlement with more than 2,500 people). Small family farms characterised American agriculture, north and south, east and west. But massive agricultural changes were taking place. Between 1840 and 1860 the production of food in America increased four fold. This was largely due to the opening up of vast new tracts of land in the west. Cereals were grown for eastern and European markets. Eastern farmers, realising they could not compete with western grain, sought new agricultural opportunities created by the growing urban markets. Many turned to dairy farming, fruit and vegetables.

Commercial farming encouraged the development of more scientific techniques including fertilisation and crop rotation. Many improvements resulted from individual experimentation but new journals informed readers of modern farming practices. Farmers also increasingly used new machines. By the end of the 1850s McCormick's

Company in Illinois was selling an average of 25,000 mechanized reapers a year. A 'scientific' farmer in 1850 could produce two to four times as much per acre as his unscientific counter-part had done in 1820.

Massive changes in transport help explain the agricultural - and industrial - changes that were underway. In 1840 it took two weeks (and often longer) to travel from New York to Chicago. By 1860 the same journey took two days or less. Transportation improved in several significant ways. The building of a number of great turnpike roads in the early nineteenth century had considerable effect. The development of steamboats revolutionised travel on the great rivers of the USA. By 1850 there were over 700 steamships operating on the Mississippi and its tributaries. Travel on the river steamships could be dangerous: over 30 per cent of those built were lost in one way or another. Nevertheless, steamships played an essential role in opening up the West. The USA also developed an impressive canal system. By 1840 the country had some 3,326 miles of canals. The most impressive was the 363 mile long Erie Canal, linking the Great Lakes to the Hudson river. However, by 1850 canals were facing great competition from railways (or railroads in American terminology). These developed at much the same time as in Britain. By 1840 the USA already had over 3,000 miles of track. By 1860 this had increased to over 30,000 miles - more track than the rest of the world combined. Railway building was financed by private capital (especially European investment) and generous city, state and federal land grants to railway companies: a few states even built and operated railways themselves. Railway companies sprouted here, there and everywhere, and there was little that was at all methodical in the way that

State	1850	1860	Increased 1850-60	Investment per mile	Gauge
Virginia	481	1731	1250	$36,679	4'85"
North Carolina	283	937	654	$18,796	4'85"
South Carolina	289	973	654	$22,675	5'0"
Georgia	643	1420	777	$20,696	5'0"
Florida	21	402	381	$21,356	5'0"
Tennessee	-	1253	1253	$24,677	5'0"
Alabama	183	743	560	$25,022	5'0"
Mississippi	75	862	787	$27,982	5'0"
Louisiana	80	335	255	$35,988	5'6"
Arkansas	-	38	38	$30,394	5'6"
Texas	-	307	307	$36,706	5'6"
Total	2055	9001	6946		

Table 1. Railway construction in the south during the 1850s (in miles)

lines developed. Some cities were linked by several competing lines. Others were not directly linked at all. To make matters worse, different railway companies used a variety of different gauges. But for all the early problems, railways helped move goods and people cheaply over great distances. As the railways followed - or led - settlers westwards, they exerted enormous influence. Their routes could determine whether a city or even a farm survived.

The development of the electric telegraph also had a major impact on American communications. Developed initially to improve railway safety, its greater potential was quickly realised. In the 1840s the American Samuel Morse devised a simple system of telegraph communication. His Morse code was soon in use all over America and the world. The electric telegraph made it possible for San Francisco (on the Pacific) to communicate directly with New York (on the Atlantic). By 1860 the USA had over 50,000 miles of telegraph and efforts had already been made to lay a telegraph cable across the Atlantic to Britain.

A growing food supply and an improved transportation system encouraged - and were encouraged by - industrial development. America's industrial 'revolution' very much mirrored that of Britain. There were important technological developments in textiles, coal, iron and steel and in the use of steam power. New machines were introduced and constantly improved. The USA was fortunate in that it had colossal mineral wealth. It could also count on massive British investment.

By the mid-nineteenth century many British observers accepted that American manufacturers operated in a way that was subtly different - and better - than their British counterparts. American industrialists, like Samuel Colt (maker of the Colt revolver), pioneered the mass production of machine-made interchangeable parts. The British dubbed this method of manufacturing 'the American system' or 'the American way'. American manufacturers seem to have been more entrepreneurial, more prepared to gamble, and more receptive to change than most of their British contemporaries. There was little labour opposition to technological innovations. Indeed it was often American workers who came up with new ideas to improve both machinery and efficiency.

The growth of industry inevitably led to increased urbanisation. In 1820 less than 10 per cent of Americans lived in towns: 20 per cent did so by 1860. Some cities experienced spectacular growth. Chicago, a town of only 40 people in 1830 had over 109,000 in 1860. Buffalo, Cleveland and Detroit all doubled their populations in successive decades. New York had over 800,000 inhabitants by 1860. Moving to the city was a form of pioneering - exhilarating but also unsettling - for many farm-born-and-raised Americans. But the growth of cities was further encouraged by a huge influx of Irish immigrants who emigrated to the USA, largely as a result of the Irish potato famine in the 1840s. The flood of immigrants led to increasing unrest. Many native Americans felt that traditional American values were being threatened.

In many cities there was ethnic unrest and frequent riots. However, by no means all Americans opposed immigration. On the contrary, some gloried in it. 'We are not a narrow tribe of men whose blood has been debased by maintaining an exclusive succession among ourselves', wrote the novelist Herman Melville. 'No: our blood is as the flood of the Amazon, made up of a thousand noble currents all pouring into one'.

The USA's economic success dazzled foreigners and Americans alike. However, it was not total. Some Americans benefited more than others and there was a widening gap between the 'haves' and 'have nots'. Moreover, expansion was cyclical. Financial panics and depressions punctuated the era. Racial, ethnic and religious diversity made it difficult for the working class to unite and organise. Less than 1 per cent of the work force belonged to a trade union in the 1840s.

5 Religion and the Reform Impulse

Mid-nineteenth century America was a religious society and the Church had a powerful effect on people's lives. Although Catholic Church membership was growing as a result of immigration, most Americans were Protestants. The major Protestant denominations were the Baptists, Methodists, Unitarians, Presbyterians and Episcopalians. Most Protestant ministers still preached a gospel of hard-work, thrift and self-discipline, and worldly success was interpreted as a sign of God's favour. In the first decades of the nineteenth century, however, there was a fervent upsurge in evangelical Protestantism. This is known as the Second Great Awakening. Preachers like Charles Finney fired up men and women to do battle against the sins of the world. The new evangelical creed rejected Calvinism and its notion of predestination: its essential message was that each individual was capable of working out his or her own salvation. If people were able to perfect themselves, it followed that they ought to do so. Moreover, they ought also to work zealously to perfect society.

'In the History of the world, the doctrine of Reform had never such scope as at the present hour', declared the writer and intellectual Ralph Waldo Emerson in 1840. Given the religious mood of moral perfectionism, many Americans were anxious to save - or at least improve - the world by stamping out every form of evil. However, not all reformers were spurred by religious motivation. Some were indifferent or even hostile to revivalism: they saw themselves as more 'scientific'. Optimistic about man's ability to control his destiny, scientific reformers were convinced that society could be changed for the better and that heaven could be created on earth. Reformers had a variety of - often over-lapping - concerns. These included temperance (by 1834 the American Society for Promotion of Temperance, dedicated to total abstinence, had over 1,000,000 members); education reform; prison reform; pacifism; women's rights; and the establishment of model co-operative communities. The most influential reform movement, however, was the anti-slavery abolitionist movement (see Chapter 3). Most of those involved in reform movements were middle-class men and women with sufficient income and leisure time to devote to good causes. Reform activists sometimes co-operated with politicians (more usually with Whigs than with Democrats) but their primary allegiance was usually to their cause rather than to a political party. The reform movements were strongest in New England, up-state New York and in the Ohio Valley. They were weakest in the South.

6 Sectionalism

The United States had never been particularly united. For much of the early nineteenth century, for example, there were rivalries between the newer states in the West and the older established states in the East. Far more important, however, were the differences between North and South. Rivalries between these two sections had existed since the start of the 'great experiment'. But by the mid-nineteenth century, North-South rivalries were threatening to break up the Union. Some historians have underplayed the differences between North and South, stressing instead the similarities between the two sections: the common language; the shared religion; the same legal and political assumptions; and the celebration of the same history. Most white Northerners and Southerners even held similar racial views, considering themselves racially superior to free or enslaved African Americans.

Other historians, however, believe that there were deep social and economic divisions between North and South - divisions which helped bring about war. Marxist historians once claimed that the Civil War was a conflict between a feudal South, still dependent on plantation agriculture, and a capitalist, industrial North. Charles Beard and other 'progressive' historians writing in the 1920s held similar views. However, the Marxist/'progressive' image of a backward, agrarian, planter-dominated South facing a modern, urban, industrialised and more egalitarian North is far too sweeping. Historians now stress that there was not one but many 'Souths' encompassing several geographical regions, each with different economic bases and different social structures. Long-established eastern states like Virginia were very different from new western states like Arkansas. The lower (or Deep) South was similarly different from the upper South. Even in the lower South, coastal plain areas were very different to upland areas. In consequence, it is difficult to generalise about the 'Old' South.

There were also many 'Norths'. Moreover, in many respects, those 'Norths' were not dissimilar economically to the 'Souths'. The ante-bellum North was industrialising, not industrialised. Only four Northern manufacturing industries employed over 50,000 people. (The biggest Northern industry was boot and shoe making.) Nor was the

North very urbanised. In 1860 only one in four Northerners lived in 'towns' with a population of more than 2,500 people. Five Northern states had no town over 20,000 people. The North (particularly the North-west) was still overwhelmingly rural.

Nor was the North much more 'bourgeois' or egalitarian than the South. In 1860 the wealthiest 10 per cent of Northerners and Southerners owned over 65 per cent of the wealth. In 1860, in both North and South, half of the free adult males held under 1 per cent of real and personal property. Both Northern and Southern whites lived in a stratified society in which there were great inequalities in status, material conditions and opportunity. That said, the typical Northerner was a native-born, self-sufficient yeoman farmer, owning 50-500 acres. And the same was true of the South! 75 per cent of Southern families in 1860 did not own slaves.

The notion that the South was economically backward can easily be challenged. In the mid-nineteenth century 'Cotton was King': cotton sales invariably making up at least 50 per cent of the USA's total exports. Many Southerners prospered as a result - just as some countries today prosper from having large oil reserves. Cotton ensured that white Southern society was fluid, mobile and enterprising. Southerners, with an eye on world cotton markets, had no option but to be entrepreneurial. Many Southerners, like Northerners, headed west to try to make their - cotton - fortune. While the population of South Carolina grew by 5 per cent in the 1850s, that of Texas leapt by 184 per cent. Trade in cotton ensured that most Southerners had an economic interest in a good railway and telegraph network. Nor was the South totally lacking in industry. In Richmond, for example, Joseph Anderson guided the Tredegar Iron Works to success. By 1840 it ranked fourth among the nation's producers of iron products.

It has sometimes been claimed that the South was dominated by a reactionary planter class. (Planters were usually defined as owning 20 or more slaves.) The planters, who made up under 5 per cent of the white population, certainly owned the South's best farmland and the major portion of its wealth, including the majority of its slaves. The Marxist historian Eugene Genovese thought this group had developed 'class cohesion and consciousness'. Genovese was certain that the planters led Southern politics and set the tone of social life. Certainly the planters did exert a disproportionate amount of political power and social influence in states such as Virginia and South Carolina. However, the situation was not much different in the North. Here, too, a small minority of wealthy men wielded considerable political and social power. Most of the men who held political office in both the North and the South were lawyers, merchants, businessmen and relatively large property owners. (In the South, this inevitably meant that most were slaveholders.) Wealthy Americans, whether in the North or South, found it easier to involve themselves in politics than the poor: they were better educated and could find the time and money to pursue their 'hobby' or 'conviction'.

The notion that the planters were a fixed 'class' - or caste - is mistaken. As in the North, there was fluidity in Southern society. Men rose and fell. Sons and daughters of planters did not automatically become planters themselves - or even own slaves, although this was usually their ambition. Many went West to realise it. There were opportunities for self-made men to become planters - and then, perhaps, to involve themselves in politics. Of the eight governors of Virginia in the two decades before the Civil War, only one had been born a planter. Three had risen from relative obscurity: one had been a tailor.

Southern states were as democratic as Northern states. Given the wide electorate, planters could not count on political dominance. If they involved themselves in politics (and by no means all did), they had to appeal to large electorates. Nor did planters speak with one voice. Some were Whigs and some were Democrats. They were thus not a cohesive class. In fact, it was small - rather than great - slaveholders who dominated Southern politics. In 1860 slaveholders held a majority of seats in all but two Southern states. But planters only held the majority of seats in one state - South Carolina.

However, there is no doubt that there were key economic and social differences between the North and the South. The North WAS more industrial than the South. The Southern states, with about 35 per cent of the USA's population, produced only about 10 per cent of the nation's manufactured output in the 1850s. In 1860 the state of Massachusetts produced more manufactured goods than all the future Confederate states combined. The North had twice as much railway track as the South. It was also far more urban. In 1860 the Confederate states had only 20 towns over 5,000 people. Even cities like Charleston, and Richmond had populations of under 40,000. Only New Orleans with 175,000 inhabitants was comparable to Northern cities in size and diversity. Equally significant was the absence of small towns in the South and the fact that most of the larger towns were on the periphery of the region (usually near the coast). Only one Southerner in fourteen was a town dweller compared with one in three people in the North.

Unlike the South, the North had a growing number of immigrants. Between 1830 and 1860 most of the 5,000,000 people emigrating from Europe to the USA settled in the North. The result was that one in six Northerners in 1860 was foreign-born and another one in six was first generation American. By contrast only one in thirty Southerners was born outside the USA. Compared to the North, where ethnic diversity was an important influence in virtually every sphere of life, Southerners lived in a world where values and institutions reflected a uniquely American experience.

The two sections did have different economic interests. The tariff was a source of constant grievance to most Southerners, who argued it benefitted Northern industrialists at the expense of Southern farmers. Southern politicians constantly pressed for free trade and complained that their section was being economically exploited by the North. In fact the South had little reason for complaint. The compromise tariff of 1833, passed after South Carolina had threatened to secede from the Union (the affair is known as the Nullification Crisis), went far to meet Southern wishes and every subsequent revision of custom duties until the Civil War was in a downward direction. But the South felt exploited in other ways. By the mid-nineteenth century, Southerners depended upon Northern credit to finance the growing of cotton, tobacco, sugar and rice: they relied upon Northerners to market these goods; and they were reliant on Northern vessels to transport them. Inevitably much of the profits from 'King Cotton' ended up in Yankee pockets.

There were other differences. Northerners were better educated than Southerners for the simple reason that there were more schools in the North. Some Southern politicians were concerned at this development and efforts were made to improve educational provision in many Southern states in the 1850s. However, the South's low population density made it difficult to provide schools for all children and many self-sufficient yeoman farmers, who saw little purpose in formal schooling, opposed paying higher taxes to fund education. By 1860 the South had only about half the North's proportion of white children enrolled in public and private schools and the proportion of illiterate whites was thus three times greater in the South than the North.

The North was far more responsive to new ideas. In the early and mid-nineteenth century it was Northerners who espoused movements for reform. Southerners, in contrast, invariably condemned all radical 'isms' - associating them with abolitionism and viewing them as a threat to the old values and institutions (not least slavery). Certain topics in the South (like slavery) were taboo: there was an 'intellectual blockade' and effectively no freedom of speech or press. Not unnaturally, Northerners saw Southerners as backward and out of touch with nineteenth century ideas and ideals.

The South was a more violent than the North. Southern whites were far more likely to carry weapons and to use them against other human beings. In 1850 there was as much recorded violence in Mississippi as in all the New England states put together and yet Mississippi's population was only a fraction that of New England. Duelling, which had died out in the North, was still fairly common in the South.

Many Southerners were concerned at the way that North and South were growing apart. Some felt threatened by the North's economic advance, fearing the South could become little more than a colony of the North. In 1851 a newspaper in Alabama published a bitter inventory of the ways in which the South was exploited:

1 We purchase all our luxuries and necessities from the North. Our

slaves are clothed with Northern manufactured goods, have Northern hats and shoes, work with Northern hoes, ploughs and other implements. The slaveholder dresses in Northern goods, 5 rides in a Northern saddle, sports his Northern carriage, reads Northern books. In Northern vessels his products are carried to market, his cotton is ginned with Northern gins, his sugar is crushed and preserved with Northern machinery, his rivers are navigated by Northern steamboats. His son is educated at a 10 Northern college, his daughter receives the finishing polish at a Northern seminary; his doctor graduates at a Northern medical college, his schools are furnished with Northern teachers, and he is furnished with Northern inventions.

Some Southerners tried to improve this state of affairs. From the early 1840s Southern newspapers, journals and commercial conventions began stressing the need for the Southern economy to diversify. The message had some effect. Southerners did invest in non-agricultural pursuits. A great deal of money was invested in railways with the result that in the 1850s the slave states more than quadrupled their railway mileage. There was an increase in the South's manufacturing industry. Nevertheless, the South fell even further behind the North industrially in the 1850s as Southerners continued to put the bulk of their capital into the production of cotton.

Many Southern whites were not concerned by the economic situation. Cotton ensured their prosperity. Given that cotton and slave prices were rising for much of the 1850s, investment in slaves and cotton seemed sensible. Many Southerners, disliking what they saw in the North, had no wish to industrialise and urbanise. There was a general Southern belief that old agrarian ways and values were better than Yankee materialism. Southerners remained proudly and defiantly rooted in the past. Many held a 'romantic' view of the Southern way of life, seeing themselves as gracious, hospitable and charitable. Yankees, in contrast, were seen as coarse, ill-mannered, aggressive and hypocritical. One Alabama politician said:

> We want no manufacturers; we desire no trading, no mechanical or manufacturing classes. As long as we have our rice, our sugar, our tobacco and our cotton, we can command wealth to purchase all we want.

The historian Wyatt Brown has claimed that Southerners were more concerned about their personal, family, community and ultimately sectional honour than Northerners. In his view, Southern white males demonstrated a sensitivity to personal insult and dreaded public humiliation. They reacted violently to even trivial incidents: there was an emphasis on personal redress of grievances, including resorting to duelling or enforcing 'shot-gun' marriages. Slaveholders were particularly concerned about their honour. Many considered themselves as descendants of the Cavaliers and held a romantic notion of Cavalier virtues including a devotion to proper manners. It should be said that many Northerners held similar views - even if they were no longer ready to fight duels. Wyatt Brown, however, may be correct in asserting that a slave society is more likely to be concerned with matters of honour than a free society: slave-owners, after all, expected that their slaves would show them both honour and respect. Non-slaveholding Southern whites expected similar treatment from blacks.

The main difference between North and South - a difference which to a large extent accounted for the socio-economic and cultural differences - was that the Northern states by the mid nineteenth century were free states and the Southern states still had slavery. Slavery was the fundamental problem. It was not a new problem. It had been a problem in 1787 when the Founding Fathers had drawn up the Constitution. It remained a problem thereafter. By the second decade of the nineteenth century Northern states had freed their slaves and large numbers of Northerners had begun to question the morality of slavery. Southern states on the other hand had invested more capital in their 'peculiar institution'. It was not only the South's capital that was tied up with slavery: its system of agriculture was based upon it; and its social system was founded upon it. For the majority of white Southerners (who did not own slaves) slavery was the best method of controlling blacks, for whom most whites had an abiding abhorrence. Slavery was the main reason for the growth of sectionalism: it under-pinned most of - if not all - the other differences between North and South.

7 Conclusion

In urbanisation, industrialisation, demographic structures, education and attitudes towards change, contemporaries were aware that there were significant differences between North and South - differences that were growing as the North's industrial development outstripped that of the South. The North was changing: the South, on the other hand, resisted change and tried to stay the same. (Most nineteenth century European travellers thought they were travelling back in time when they visited the South: it was a totally different environment from the bustling North.) By 1850 Southerners were becoming increasingly conscious of their distinct 'Southerness'. North and South might speak the same language - but (as James McPherson has pointed out) they were increasingly using this language to revile each other. The shared commitment to Protestantism had become a divisive rather than a unifying factor with most of the major denominations splitting by the 1840s into hostile Southern and Northern branches over the question of slavery. Even the shared commitment to republicanism was divisive.

Many Northerners interpreted this as a commitment to abolish slavery: most Southerners, on the other hand, continued to insist that one of the most cherished tenets of republican liberty was the right to own slave property.

By the mid-nineteenth century there was a widening disparity in numbers and strength between North and South. In 1790 the population of the Northern and Southern states had been about equal. But by 1850 Northerners outnumbered Southerners by a ratio of more than 3 to 2. This meant that Northern states had more seats in the House of Representatives than Southern states. In consequence, Southerners, increasingly aware of the danger of becoming a permanent minority, were determined to try to maintain a position of equality in the Senate. This meant that westward expansion was a crucial issue. If new Western states entered the Union as free states it was possible that slavery would be declared illegal by a Northern-dominated Congress.

Making notes on *'The USA in the Mid-nineteenth Century'*

Your notes on this chapter should give you a basic understanding of the political, economic and social situation in the USA in the mid-nineteenth century and enable you to answer the following questions: 1 How did the American Constitution operate? 2 What were the main features of American politics? 3 What were the main differences between the Whigs and Democrats? 4 Was the USA a 'society of equals'? 5 What were the main economic developments in the USA in the early nineteenth century? 6 What were the main religious and reform developments? 7 In what sense were North and South similar - and different?

Source-based questions on *'The USA in the Mid-nineteenth Century'*

1 Democracy in Action
Read the account of democracy at grass roots level on page 6. Answer the following questions:
a) Is the account written by an American or a European? Explain your answer. (2 marks)
b) Why was the Presidential appointment of postmasters important in mid-nineteenth century America? (3 marks)
c) What arguments might a supporter of American democracy have used to extol its virtues? (5 marks)
d) How might a critic of American democracy have responded? (5 marks)

2 Southern Economic Development
Read the Alabamian account on pages 20-21 and examine the railway

construction statistics on page 14. Answer the following questions:
a) Which Southern states seem to have been the most developed? (2 marks)
b) What problems would have been caused by the different railway gauges? (2 marks)
c) Account for the different costs of investment per mile. (3 marks)
d) What does the railway construction programme suggest about the Southern economy in the 1850s? (5 marks)
e) Does the railway construction bear out the views of the Alabama editor (3 marks)

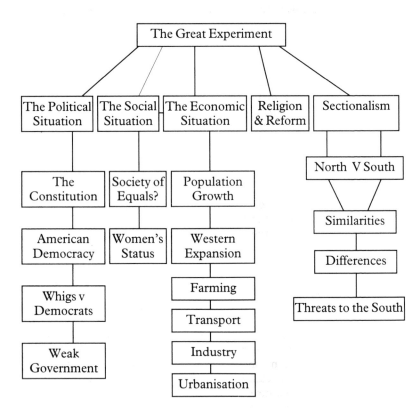

Summary - The USA in the Mid-nineteenth Century

CHAPTER 3

The Peculiar Institution

1 Introduction

The settlement of North America in the seventeenth century was not purely a European enterprise. In 1619, a year before the Pilgrim Fathers set sail in the 'Mayflower', John Rolfe in Virginia reported 'about the last of August came in a Dutch man-of-war that sold us 20 negars'. This is the first record of Africans 'settling' in America. As the extract makes clear, the 20 Africans in 1619 did not cross the Atlantic by choice. They came as slaves. This was the experience of virtually all Africans who were shipped to North America in the seventeenth and eighteenth centuries. In 1808 the United States declared the African slave trade illegal. But by then there were hundreds of thousands of slaves already in the USA and the slave population continued to expand naturally. By 1860 there were some 4,000,000 slaves and slavery had become the main problem dividing Americans. Problems associated with slavery continue to divide historians: indeed perhaps no issue in American history has generated quite as many interpretations or as much controversy. This chapter will examine some of those controversies.

2 The Growth of Slavery

Historians continue to debate the nature of the West African background from which the vast majority of slaves came. Until this century historians invariably assumed that background to be both primitive and savage. But late twentieth century historians have stressed the fact that there were several distinct, diverse and often sophisticated West African tribal cultures. Most seventeenth and eighteenth century Europeans would have insisted that Africans were better off as slaves in America than as slaves (or even free men!) in Africa. Present day historians are far from convinced. Historians also debate the effects of transportation across the Atlantic. Some think the horrors of the Middle Passage, followed by the shock of being sold into slavery, had such an impact on most Africans that they were left totally uprooted and de-culturised. But others claim that African Americans retained certain features of their native culture.

There is also debate about precisely when, how and why slavery developed. Some historians think that in the first part of the seventeenth century the (relatively few) Africans who came to America were indentured servants rather than slaves. But most are convinced that, whatever their precise legal status, Africans were, from the start, effectively slaves. After 1660 there is no doubt that the Africans who came to North America came as slaves. Colonial legislation made it clear that Africans, unlike white indentured servants, served their owners for life and that their slave status would be passed on to their children.

The slave trade was at its height in the eighteenth century. In the four decades after 1740 over 200,000 slaves were imported to the 13 American colonies. There were good (or bad!) economic reasons for the growth of slavery. African slaves provided better labour than white indentured servants when it came to the production of tobacco (in Virginia and Maryland) and rice and indigo (in South Carolina and Georgia). Nor, could they easily escape. Whereas white indentured servants could easily merge into American society, blacks were assumed to be slaves. Few people in the eighteenth century questioned the morality of slavery: most believed that Africans were inferior. In 1776 slavery existed in all the 13 colonies. However, it was of major importance only in the South, largely because the Northern climate was not suited to plantation agriculture.

3 Slavery: 1776-c1830

In the last decades of the eighteenth century some Americans began to condemn slavery. Opposition came first from radical Protestant groups, especially Quakers, who considered it a moral evil. Others saw slavery as inconsistent with enlightened ideas and (American) revolutionary ideology which stressed individual liberty, equality and democratic political participation. It was also incompatible with notions of free enterprise and free trade. Northern states, starting with Vermont in 1777, gradually abolished slavery: by 1820 it had ended in virtually all the Northern states. In 1787 Congress passed the North West Ordinance which kept slavery out of the vast North West Territory. Even some Southerners in the late eighteenth and early nineteenth centuries regarded slavery as an evil (albeit necessary) and a few, like George Washington, freed their slaves. In the early nineteenth century the American Anti-Slavery Society was strongest in the upper South.

However, the attack on slavery - and concern for black Americans - should not be over-emphasised. In Maryland and Virginia, soil depletion meant that planters could no longer produce bumper crops of tobacco. Instead they turned to less labour intensive crops like grain, fruits and vegetables. This meant there was less need for slaves. While some upper South planters freed their slaves for humane reasons, far more had economic motives. They simply did not need slaves. But if there were good economic reasons for jettisoning slavery in the upper South, there were soon far better economic reasons for maintaining it in the lower South. The main reason was the sudden expansion in the amount of cotton grown. In 1790 only 9,000 bales of cotton were produced in the United States, largely because it was difficult to separate short-fibre cotton (the only cotton which easily grew in the South) from its seed. However, the increased demand for cotton in Britain led to a rise in prices and thus increased incentive to produce. In 1793 Eli Whitney invented a cotton engine - or 'gin' - which enabled short-fibre cotton to be quickly separated from its seed. The gin, which could do the work of 50 people, revolutionised Southern agriculture. Suddenly it became highly profitable to grow cotton and Southerners cashed in. By the 1830s the South was producing 2,000,000 bales per year. By 1860 this had grown to near 5,000,000 bales. 'King Cotton' soon outstripped all other plantation crops in economic importance. From 1815 to 1860 cotton represented more than 50 per cent of all the US exports.

Such was the demand - and such the profits - that cotton production spread westwards. New plantations were created on the fertile soil of territories that became the states of Kentucky, Tennessee, Alabama, Mississippi, Arkansas and Texas. Cotton production needed a large amount of unskilled labour. Slave labour was ideal. Cotton and slavery, therefore, were interlinked. By 1860 over 50 per cent of all American slaves were employed in growing and picking cotton. Southerners migrating westwards either took their slaves with them or purchased surplus 'stock' from the upper South.

Most Southerners in the late eighteenth and early nineteenth centuries remained totally committed to their peculiar institution. The Founding Fathers in 1787 had realised they could not tamper with slavery in the South. While they had avoided using the word 'slave', they accepted and acknowledged the existence of slavery. Slaves were accepted - for representation and taxation purposes - as three-fifths of a free person. The Constitution also made clear that slaves who fled to a free state were still slaves and liable to be returned to bondage. In 1793 Congress enacted a Fugitive Slave Law whereby slave owners were authorised to recapture their escaped slaves beyond the state lines. White Southerners do not seem to have experienced any real crisis of confidence in slavery. Few saw it as an evil. Events in Haiti in the 1790s, where slaves had won their freedom, massacring most of the white population in the process, and setting up a corrupt and savage black republic, convinced most Southerners that slavery must be maintained as a means of race control. The rise of militant abolitionism in the North in the 1830s made Southerners even more determined to maintain slavery.

4 The Abolitionists

Most abolitionists in the first two decades of the nineteenth century supported gradual emancipation, with financial compensation for the slaveowners. They also believed that freed slaves should be encouraged to return to Africa. The American Colonisation Society, established in 1817, supported this aim. In 1822 the USA actually purchased Liberia, a small area on the west coast of Africa, as a suitable base for returning African Americans. This policy, however, had relatively little success.

Only 10,000 blacks had returned to Africa by 1860: in the same period the United States' slave population increased by about 2,000,000. There was never enough funds to free - and then transport - more than a fraction of the slaves. Moreover, most ex-slaves were - and regarded themselves as - native Americans: they were as unsuited to life in Africa as most American whites. The African colonisation idea thus attracted little black support.

In the early 1830s a new and far more strident abolitionist movement developed. This was associated with a fervent young Bostonian, William Lloyd Garrison. Convinced that slavery was both a sin and a crime, Garrison totally rejected the notion of gradual emancipation, colonisation and compensation, and demanded (without any notion of how it should be done) immediate abolition. In January 1831 Garrison launched a new abolitionist journal, 'The Liberator'. 'I do not wish to think or speak or write with moderation', declared Garrison. 'I am in earnest - I will not equivocate - I will not excuse - I will not retreat a single inch - AND I WILL BE HEARD!'

Garrison was - and remains - a controversial character. His supporters saw him as a dedicated idealist. His critics - and there were many both in the North and South - regarded him as a vain and self-righteous bigot. For the next four decades he was to be one of the leading abolitionists. (Like many abolitionists he was involved in other reform movements, including pacifism, temperance and women's rights: he was also an enthusiastic spiritualist!) Garrison's influence, however, has sometimes been exaggerated. He was just one among many men and women who committed their lives to the cause of abolition. 'The Liberator's' circulation never exceeded 3,000 - 75 per cent of whom were free blacks. Many free blacks - and white abolitionists for that matter - had long held views similar to those which Garrison now propounded. His words, therefore, fell on receptive ears.

In 1832 a militant New England Anti-Slavery Society was established. This was followed a year later by the National Anti-Slavery Society. By 1838 the Society had nearly 250,000 members. Abolitionists, helped by the new steam press, were soon churning out a mass of anti-slavery literature. They also organised frequent and massive petitions to Congress. To prevent North-South division, Congress introduced the 'gag rule' in 1836 which ensured that abolitionist petitions were not discussed.

Historians have tried to explain why the abolitionist movement suddenly became so strong in the North in the 1830s. Some stress that it was part of a world-wide phenomenon, in which Britain in particular played an important role. British anti-slavery writings in the 1820s certainly had a receptive audience in the USA. (Britain itself actually abolished slavery throughout its colonies in 1833.) Other historians have stressed native American roots and emphasised the importance of the religious revival in the first three decades of the nineteenth century.

Certainly many of the leading abolitionists were evangelical Protestants who believed that people should do battle against the sins of the world. However, the Protestant Churches did not rally behind abolition as strongly as they rallied behind temperance.

The abolitionists, themselves, are difficult to categorise. Some were conservative; others radical. Many were deeply religious but others were prompted more by 'scientific' concern. If anything the abolitionist movement was more urban than rural: it was strongest in New England, in New York and in the Ohio Valley. Most of its leaders were well-educated, fairly wealthy and often from distinguished families. Women played a crucial role. So too did free blacks, some of whom, like Frederick Douglass, were ex-slaves. 'I appear this evening as a thief and robber', Douglass told Northern audiences. 'I stole this head, these limbs, this body from my master and ran off with them'. It was once common place for historians to portray the - white - abolitionists as a displaced elite, victims of the industrial revolution who were losing status and who found an outlet for their internal psychological problems and status anxieties in a crusade against slavery. This view is now seen as far too simplistic. In reality, abolitionists had very different economic, social and cultural backgrounds, very varied personalities, and a host of reasons for devoting (at least part of) their lives to the abolitionist cause.

Historians have often praised the abolitionists' moral courage and dedicated idealism. (Historians tend to approve people in the past who held values akin to twentieth century values!) But some have been critical, pointing out that many abolitionists were fanatics and 'holier than thou' rabble rousers. Many white abolitionists had a condescending attitude - and sometimes even an antipathy - to blacks. Local anti-slavery societies often provided less than full membership rights for blacks and some white abolitionists were opposed to full equality for blacks.

The extent of the abolitionists' success must not be exaggerated. The movement had only limited appeal in the North. Racism continued to remain strong in the North. In the 1830s the French writer De Tocqueville commented: 'The prejudice of race appears to be stronger in the states that have abolished slavery than in those where it still exists and nowhere is it so intolerant as in those states where servitude has never existed'. Many Northerners, fearing a northern exodus of liberated slaves and fearful of the effect that the new crusade would have in the South, hated the abolitionists. In consequence, they were frequently attacked, both in print and physically. Anti-slavery meetings (and abolitionist printing presses) were sometimes broken up by angry Northern mobs. Garrison came close to being lynched in Boston. In 1837 Elijah Lovejoy became the first abolitionist martyr when he was murdered by a mob in Illinois.

The abolitionists also had little political success. Failing to win the support of either the Whig or Democrat party, abolitionists set up their own party - the Liberty party. James Birney, the Liberty party presidential candidate, received only 7,000 votes (0.3 per cent of the total) in 1840. Not all abolitionists supported the establishment of the Liberty party. There were great disagreements about what tactics should be used. Some favoured direct action and supported trying to initiate a slave revolt in the South. Others, while accepting that the slaves had every right to revolt, argued (sensibly) that a slave insurrection would be disastrous for the slaves. Some, opposed to any violence, favoured 'moral' rather than 'physical' force and hoped to win white support in the South. Garrison was ready to argue that the North should break with the South in order to avoid all responsibility for slavery. The plethora of different opinion, coupled with individual feuds and hostility (many abolitionists disliked Garrison's enthusiasm for women's rights both within and outside the anti-slavery movement), resulted in a major schism in the American Anti-Slavery Society in 1840.

The abolitionists main failure, however, was in the South. Here they had no success whatsoever in winning white support. Just the reverse! They were not helped by the fact that in 1831 (the same year as Garrison's 'The Liberator' began), there was a serious slave revolt in Virginia. This was led by Nat Turner. A well-educated and articulate slave, Turner managed to win the support of about 70 slaves and killed 55 whites (mainly women and children) before being captured and executed. This revolt appalled white Southerners. Fear of slave insurrection wasalmost endemic in the South. Most Southerners blamed Northern abolitionists for stirring up trouble among the slaves.

The abolitionists' attacks on slavery goaded Southerners to extol the virtues of their peculiar institution. A clutch of Southern writers now argued that slavery was a positive good rather than a necessary evil. History, religion, anthropology and economics were all used to defend slavery. All the great civilisations in the past, it was claimed, had been based on slavery or serfdom. The Bible seemed to sanction bondage. At no point did Christ actually condemn slavery. Indeed he seemed to approve it. Blacks were depicted as an inferior species - physically, intellectually and emotionally. Some pro-slavers thought they had been cast out by God. Many claimed slaves were child-like creatures, incapable of taking responsibility for themselves. Protected by paternalistic slaveholders, they were better off than most working men in Northern factories or freed blacks in Haiti or Africa. Slavery in the USA, was portrayed as the most beneficial form of slavery that had ever existed. Abolitionists were depicted as irresponsible revolutionaries bent on destroying the American republic.

As well as vigorously defending slavery both in print and in words, Southerners also took specific action against abolitionists. Abolitionist literature was excluded from most Southern states. In some states the penalty for circulating 'incendiary' literature among blacks was death. From the early 1830s it was dangerous for anyone to express anti-slavery opinions in the South. Some states passed laws limiting the freedom of speech. Those suspected of having abolitionist sympathies were driven out, often after being tarred and feathered. A number of Southern states put a price on the head of Garrison and other leading reformers.

The white South, slaveholders and non-slaveholders alike, was united in its resistance to Northern abolitionism. The abolitionist crusade, therefore, had little immediate impact on the slaves: if anything, it perhaps made their position worse. Many Southern states placed new restrictions on slaves and there was less talk of the possibility of gradual emancipation. Nevertheless, if the abolitionists did little in the short term to help the slaves, they did a great deal to polarise American opinion and to heighten sectional animosity. They stirred the consciences of an increasing number of Northerners and succeeded in keeping slavery in the forefront of public attention. The gag rule and Southern interference with freedom of speech seemed proof of the growing pernicious influence of the Slave Power. Southerners, while greatly exaggerating the extent of Northern support for abolitionism, correctly sensed that Northern opinion had a growing affinity for anti-slavery doctrines. By the 1850s many Northerners did believe that slavery was an unnecessary evil. Most white Southerners, on the other hand, considered it a necessary good.

5 The Nature of the Peculiar Institution

Slavery in the USA reached its prime in the period 1830 to 1860, expanding and flourishing in the midst of the most advanced democratic society in the world. Historians continue to debate the nature of the peculiar institution. They have a considerable number of primary sources with which to work, including plantation records, census returns, court records, newspapers, diaries, travellers' accounts and political speeches. However, there are serious gaps in the evidence. The most substantial records come from the great plantations. Much less was written about slavery in families which had under five slaves. Moreover, there is limited evidence from the slaves themselves, few of whom could read and write. The best nineteenth century accounts of what it was like to experience slavery were written by fugitive slaves, some of whom became leading abolitionists. But such men and women were probably not typical slaves. There are large numbers of reminiscences resulting from interviews with former slaves, conducted in the late 1930s. But these accounts are flawed by the fact that those who provided their recollections had only experienced slavery as children and had hazy memories of what life was like.

Historians have interpreted the (sometimes conflicting) sources in a variety of (often conflicting) ways. One major problem facing historians is that slavery changed over time: it was not necessarily the same in the 1830s as it was in the 1850s. Moreover, it also varied considerably from place to place. Slavery in Delaware, where only one family in 30 owned a slave, was very different from slavery in South Carolina, where one family in two owned a slave. But a slave's experience in Delaware (or South Carolina) very much depended on the slaveowner. In consequence, generalisations are difficult to make and exceptions can be found to almost every rule. Perhaps the only thing that can be said with certainty is that slavery was a system of many systems.

The United States census returns of 1850 and 1860 provide a starting point for trying to understand the nature of the peculiar institution. In 1850 there were about 3,200,000 slaves (compared to 6,200,000 whites) and some 228,000 free blacks in the 15 Southern slave states. By 1860 there were nearly 4,000,000 slaves (compared to some 8,000,000 whites) and about 250,000 free blacks in the South. The slaves were concentrated mainly in the lower South. Slaves actually outnumbered whites in South Carolina and Mississippi. There were far fewer slaves in the upper South. In 1850 one in three white Southern families owned slaves. By 1860 only 385,000 of the 1,500,000 white families did so: that is about one family in four. The rising cost of slaves in the 1850s was one reason for the decline in the number of slaveowners. This decline worried some Southern politicians who believed that the South would be more united if every white family owned a slave and thus had a vested interest in slavery. In 1860 88 per cent of slaveholders owned fewer than

Border slaveholding states

	WHITE	SLAVE	FREE BLACK	TOTAL
Delaware	90,589 (80.7%)	1,798 (01.6%)	19,829 (17.7%)	112,216
Kentucky	919,484 (79.6%)	225,483 (19.5%)	10,684 (00.9%)	1,155,651
Maryland	515,918 (75.1%)	87,189 (12.7%)	83,942 (12.2%)	687,049
Missouri	1,063,489 (90.0%)	114,931 (09.7%)	3,572 (00.3%)	1,181,992
Total	2,589,480 (82.5%)	429,401 (13.7%)	118,027 (3.8%)	3,136,908

Eleven future Confederate states

	WHITE	SLAVE	FREE BLACK	TOTAL
Alabama	526,271 (54.6%)	435,080 (45.1%)	2,690 (00.3%)	964,041
Arkansas	324,143 (74.4%)	111,115 (25.5%)	114 (00.1%)	435,402
Florida	77,747 (55.4%)	61,745 (44.0%)	932 (00.7%)	140,424
Georgia	591,550 (56.0%)	462,198 (43.7%)	3,500 (00.3%)	1,057,248
Louisiana	357,456 (50.5%)	331,726 (46.9%)	18,647 (02.6%)	707,829
Mississippi	353,899 (44.7%)	436,631 (55.2%)	773 (00.1%)	791,303
North Carolina	629,942 (63.5%)	331,059 (33.4%)	30,463 (03.1%)	991,464
South Carolina	291,300 (41.4%)	402,406 (57.2%)	9,914 (01.4%)	703,620
Tennessee	826,722 (74.5%)	275,719 (24.9%)	7,300 (00.7%)	1,109,741
Texas	420,891 (69.7%)	182,566 (30.2%)	355 (00.1%)	603,812
Virginia	1,047,299 (65.5%)	490,865 (30.8%)	58,042 (03.6%)	1,596,206
Total	5,447,220 (59.9%)	3,521,110 (38.7%)	132,760 (01.5%)	9,101,090

Table 2. Population distribution in 1860

20 slaves and 50 per cent of slaveowners owned no more than five slaves. But only about 25 per cent of slaves belonged to holders of less than ten slaves and over 50 per cent of slaves lived on plantations with over 20 slaves. In short, the 'typical' slaveholder did not own the 'typical' slave. The majority of slaves were held by about 10,000 families. 3,000 families had over 100 slaves.

75 per cent of slaves were mainly involved in agricultural work - 55 per cent were employed in cotton production, 10 per cent in tobacco and 10 per cent in sugar, rice and hemp. Some 15 per cent of slaves were domestic servants. In 1860 about 10 per cent lived in towns or worked in a variety of industries. For example, slaves were frequently employed in building Southern railways. Slaves were sometimes hired out to other employers for parts of the year. In towns, some slaves, with particular skills, hired themselves out.

6 Free Blacks

Not all African Americans were slaves. By 1860 there were about 250,000 free blacks in the South. Most lived in the upper South and cities, particularly New Orleans. A high percentage were mulattoes, who had been given their freedom by their white fathers. Southern free blacks lived in an uneasy world. They had to carry documentation proving their freedom at all times or risk the danger of being enslaved. They had no political rights and their legal status was precarious. Job opportunities for free blacks were also limited by law and custom. Nevertheless a few prospered. In Charleston in 1860 there were some 360 'coloured' taxpayers. 130 of these owned 390 slaves!

The North had some 200,000 free blacks. Their position, in many ways, was similar to that of free blacks in the South. Northern blacks usually had the worst jobs and segregation was the norm in most aspects of life. Only three Northern states allowed blacks to vote on terms of complete parity with whites in 1860. Some Northern states tried to exclude blacks altogether. However, Paul Finkelman has recently stressed that race relations in the ante-bellum North showed greater complexity and ambiguity than was once thought. A number of Northern politicians in the decades before the Civil War worked to expand black rights. By 1860 legal changes had altered the status of Northern blacks in many Northern states, often in dramatic ways. Only three free states restricted black immigration. Most Northern states did their best to protect fugitive slaves from being returned to the South. Almost all Northern states provided some public education for blacks and integrated schools existed in some states. By 1861 Northern blacks had more rights than at any time in the previous thirty years.

7 How Bad was Slavery?

Over the last century there have been major debates about whether slavery American-style was a system of ruthless exploitation or whether, on the contrary, it was a paternalistic type of welfare state, offering protection for the slaves from the cradle to the grave. (These debates began where the propaganda war between abolitionists and apologists for slavery left off!) In the first decades of the twentieth century Ulrich B. Phillips, a white Southern historian, wrote two very influential books on slavery: *American Negro Slavery* (1918) and *Life and Labour in the Old South* (1929). Phillips argued that slavery was as benign and benevolent an institution as slaveholders had always claimed it to be. Most slaves, thought Phillips, were content with their lot. Relationships between the slaves and their owners were marked by 'gentleness, kind-hearted friendship and mutual loyalty'. Phillips' view tended to be the orthodox view until the mid-twentieth century.

In 1956 Kenneth Stampp, a white Northerner, published *The Peculiar Institution* in which he put forward a very different interpretation of slavery. While accepting that there were massive variations, Stampp held that, in general, slavery was harsh rather than benign. He saw little in the way of good relationships between owner and owned. In his view, the typical plantation was an area of persistent conflict between the master and the slaves who were, quite naturally, 'a troublesome property'. Stampp's thesis, which has been supported by a host of other historians, remains the prevailing view.

However, in 1974 Fogel and Engerman produced *Time on the Cross*. The authors claimed to have used new 'cliometric' techniques. Feeding a vast amount of source material into computers, they came up with a host of statistics which, they argued, displayed precisely what slavery was like. Their conclusions, at least with regard to slave conditions, were similar to those of Phillips. In Fogel and Engerman's view, white planters were a 'rational' and humane capitalist class and slavery a mild and efficient system of labour. Slaves, said Fogel and Engerman, were controlled with minimal force and enjoyed a standard of living comparable to that of industrial workers in the North.

The response to *Time on the Cross* was overwhelmingly critical. Many historians attacked Fogel and Engerman's techniques and insisted that their conclusions did not possess the 'scientific' status that the authors claimed. Their findings, according to two critics, Sutch and Gutman, were 'confused, circular and so unsubtle as to be naive. Some of their conclusions can be disproved, while others remain unsupported conjectures, in some cases fanciful speculations'.

Those, like Phillips and Fogel and Engerman, who have argued that slavery was a reasonably benign system have generally made the following points. They claim that slaves did not necessarily work much harder or longer than most mid-nineteenth century Americans. Most did not work on Sundays, sometimes had half a day to themselves on Saturdays, and received a fair number of holidays. Much of their work was seasonal or dependent on clement weather. Floggings were rare, if only because slave owners had a vested interest in the care and maintenance of their property. Just as most Rolls Royce owners today take good care of their cars, so slave owners looked after their 'property'. (A prime field hand was worth much the same as a modern day top-of-the-range car.) Most owners preferred the carrot as a source of motivation to the stick. Slaves who worked hard were given extra holidays, more clothing and food, and often their own garden plots.

Those who have defended slave conditions have claimed that there was considerable variety in the nature and organisation of slaves' work. By no means all toiled for long hours on cotton plantations. Within slavery there was a hierarchy, tantamount to a career structure. Hard-working - or lucky - slaves had a good chance of promotion. They could pick up a skill or become a slave driver or a plantation overseer. Slaves, according to Fogel and Engerman, actually benefited from their work. They claimed that, 'Over the course of his lifetime, the typical slave field had received about 90 per cent of the income he produced'. Many slaves were thus imbibed with the Protestant work ethic. Those who were not so imbibed were at least able to modify and subvert the system. By using strategies such as feigning illness or working slowly, they were often able to convert privileges into rights.

Defenders of slavery have claimed that, given the general standards of the day, slaves were fed, clothed and housed reasonably well - and that slaves' material conditions were improving as conditions for whites also improved. Slaves, moreover, enjoyed a large measure of security. On most plantations, they did not have to worry about food, shelter, clothing and illness. Eugene Genovese (while not defending slave conditions) has argued that most plantation holders had an aristocratic code of honour. Seeing them as more paternalistic than capitalistic, he has also claimed that they were not even particularly negrophobic.

By the early nineteenth century there was no need to import African slaves. The slave population increased naturally at much the same rate as white population growth. By 1860 slaves lived almost as long as white Southerners. The slave family, far from being undermined by the slave system, was the basic unit of social organisation and there were strong ties of kinship. Slaves usually chose their own partners. It was not unusual for a slave to be traded so that a couple who were fond of each other could live together. Slave suicides were surprisingly rare. Although slaves, in strict legal terms, were regarded as 'chattels' (and thus similar to horses, tables or chairs), they were also viewed as human beings. Unlike chattels, they were held responsible for crimes. In most states they also had some legal protection, especially if mistreatment was committed by someone other than their own master. The evidence suggests that there were relatively few brutal owners. There was even relatively little sexual exploitation. Most whites were restrained in their treatment of slaves by conventional Christian morality, by their own standards of decency, by self-interest and by peer group pressure.

If slave conditions had been really bad then one would have expected a serious slave revolt to have occurred. This simply did not happen. In the nineteenth century there were only three planned revolts: that of Gabriel Prosser in 1800: that of Denmark Vesey in 1822; and that of Nat Turner in 1831. Only Nat Turner's revolt actually occurred and that was quickly put down. John Brown's attempt to stir up a slave revolt in 1859 failed miserably (see page 109-111). There was not even a slave rebellion during the Civil War. Only a few hundred slaves a year made any serious attempt to escape to freedom in the North or in Canada. Slaves could always hope for freedom. Some, particularly those in the upper South, were granted freedom by their owners. Others succeeded in making enough money to purchase their freedom. By 1860 nearly half the black population in Maryland was free. Slaves in towns often had virtual freedom, including the right to negotiate their own contracts.

However, most historians remain convinced, as nineteenth century abolitionists were convinced, that slave conditions were harsh, if not intolerable. Slaves, after all, were slaves. Their owners had unlimited power over them. They could be sold, separated from their families, punished, sexually exploited, and even killed without redress. Most lived, in consequence, in a state of constant insecurity. Firm discipline seems to have been the norm. This was an age that believed to spare the rod was to spoil the child - and slave. Floggings, brandings and mutilations were common. The threat of separating a slave from his or her family was an even more effective form of punishment and control. It is difficult to establish that most Southern planters were sincerely paternalistic. Most accepted that ultimately they ruled by fear and discipline. Virtually all held racist views.

On the whole, slaves do seem to have laboured under harsh conditions. They commonly toiled from dawn to dusk, and worked longer hours than most white Americans. The aim of most slaveowners was to make a profit - and thus to extract the maximum amount of work for the barest cost. On cotton and sugar plantations slaves usually worked in gangs supervised by a black driver and a white overseer, both of whom were quite prepared to use the whip if workers fell behind the pace. Slaves' normal diet, while being sufficient in quantity, was monotonous (corn and pork were the main components) and resulted in many slaves having vitamin deficiencies. Most slaves lived in overcrowded log cabins. They had few prospects of promotion: in most states it was illegal for them be taught to read and write.

The slave family unit was far from sacrosanct. Possibly a quarter to a third of slave marriages were broken by forced separation. In the 1850s some 250,000 slaves were taken westwards to new cotton areas. Many went as family units. But thousands of others were separated from their families. By the 1850s manumission (the granting of freedom) was far less common than it had been earlier in the century. Between 1810 and 1860 all the Southern states passed laws severely restricting the right of slave-owners to free their slaves. Even those slaves who were given their freedom were often required to leave the state in which they lived, thus abandoning their family and friends. In such circumstances, some slaves preferred not to be freed.

The fact that there were no major revolts is not proof that slaves were content with their lot. It is simply testimony to most slaves' realism. A great slave revolt was impossible to organise. Whites had far too much power. Slaves were a minority in most Southern states. They were also scattered across a huge area. They were not allowed to own horses or fire-arms. Nor were they allowed to congregate in large groups. A curfew system was often imposed at night. As the 1850s wore on restrictions on slaves tightened. White patrols policed many rural districts, ensuring that slaves were securely in their quarters. Slaves suspected of plotting rebellion faced almost certain death. A slave uprising at any time, even during the Civil War, would have been tantamount to mass suicide.

Individual slaves found it difficult to escape from slavery and it was virtually impossible for a family group to make it to freedom. Most fugitives were caught within days and severely punished. The 'underground railway', despite abolitionist propaganda and Southern fears, was far from extensive or well organised. Even those slaves who did make it to safety in the North risked the possibility of being apprehended and returned to their owners. The evidence suggests that most slaves hated slavery. Whenever they had the opportunity of freedom during the Civil War most took it.

In Stampp's view, 'The only generalisation that can be made with relative confidence is that some masters were harsh and frugal; others were mild and generous and the rest ran the whole gamut in between'. But historians do need to make generalisations. Most would probably accept household servants generally had an easier life than field hands, especially those labouring in the rice growing areas of the deep South. (An effective way to discipline a slave was to threaten to sell him or her to an owner in the deep South.) The historian Escott is inclined to the view that slaves on small farms had a worse lot than those on big plantations, if only because they spent much more time under the close supervision of their owner and had no sense of belonging to a sizeable slave community. Whether slave women had an easier - or harder - lot than slave men is a subject of some debate. It has been argued that slave women had a more dominant role than women in white society and were very much 'mistresses of their cabins'. However, most historians think that slave society echoed free society and that men usually had the primary role. Domestic chores within slave families were usually done by women on top of their heavy work for their owners.

8 How did Slavery in the USA Compare with Slavery Elsewhere?

In the mid-twentieth century, some historians and sociologists tried to compare slavery in the USA with slavery elsewhere. Attempts to compare nineteenth century American slavery with slavery in Ancient Rome are unconvincing: the two societies were so different economi-cally, socially, ideologically, technologically and culturally. However, many historians see some mileage in comparing slavery in nineteenth century America with slavery in places such as Brazil and Cuba in the same period. A number of historians have claimed that slavery in Latin America was less severe than slavery in the USA. Slaves seem to have had more legal protection. Spanish and Portuguese law, unlike American law, at least recognised the essential humanity of the black slave. So too did the Roman Catholic Church. In Brazil and Cuba slaves were baptised and thus became members of the Catholic Church. This may have offered some protection. In Latin America slaves could legally marry and possibly had more rest days. Manumission was also easier. It has also been claimed that there was less race consciousness in Latin America than in the USA. The fact that integration between the races was commoner may have led to slavery being less harsh. Blacks in Latin America were not necessarily viewed as the inferior, servile race.

However, most historians now hold the view that slaves in the USA were far better off materially than those in Cuba and Brazil. Certainly they lived longer. The natural increase of the United States' slave population was unique. In all other slave societies of the Western hemisphere, the slave population failed to reproduce itself and was sustained only by the injection of new slaves from Africa. In Latin America the system had tended to be one of ruthless exploitation of the slaves to the point of exhaustion, sickness and death, and then the replacement by fresh stock. Although slaves in Brazil and Cuba appeared to have had more in the way of legal rights and protection, in reality this meant very little. Nor did the Catholic Church do much to protect the lot of slaves. It had no better - and some would argue an even worse - record than Protestant Churches in terms of condemning slavery as an institution. There is also evidence that racism was as prevalent in Brazil and Cuba as it was in the USA. Only with regard to manumission were slaves in Brazil and Cuba better off than slaves in the USA.

9 What Effect did Slavery have on Slaves?

In his book *Slavery: a Problem in American Institutional and Intellectual Life* (1959), Stanley Elkins, making use of social psychology and personality theory, claimed that the 'closed' system of American slavery had 'noticeable effects upon the slave's very personality'. He went on to argue that, as a result of the repressive system, most American slaves displayed 'Sambo'-like traits: they were 'docile and irresponsible, loyal but lazy, humble but chronically given to lying and stealing ... full of infantile silliness'. Elkins went further. He claimed that inmates of Nazi concentration camps displayed similar characteristics. Child-like conformity was the only way that both concentration camp inmates and Southern slaves could hope to survive. Absolute power, in Elkins opinion, resulted in absolute dependency.

Elkins' thesis, while opening new avenues of historical debate, brought a critical response. Many historians were instinctively suspicious of psychological models, regarding them as inadequate substitutes for 'real' historical research. Critics pointed out that the analogy between concentration camps and the peculiar institution was not particularly apt. However bad slavery was, it did not compare with conditions in the Nazi death camps. Plantations were profit-making enterprises, not places of extermination. Nor, from the point of view of the slave, was the American South a totally closed society. There were massive variations from place to place and from time to time. Many slaves, for example, had little contact with whites. In consequence, they only occasionally had to act out the ritual of deference. Slaves on small farms usually had very different relationships with their owners. In short, the peculiar institution allowed slaves a wider opportunity for development of personality than Elkins recognised. Elkins came to regret his concentration camp analogy and accepted that 'something less than absolute power produces something less than absolute dependency'. Instead, he argued that a better analogy might have been the effects that prison, boarding school and hospital often have on inmates' characters.

A more trenchant criticism of Elkins has been the claim that most slaves did not display Sambo-like traits. The historian Blassingame thought the typical field hand was 'sullenly disobedient and hostilely submissive'. He suggested that there were at least three stereo-type slave characters. While accepting that 'Sambo'-type slaves did exist, Blassingame thought there were rebellious 'Nats' and unco-operative but generally deferential 'Jacks' (perhaps the majority). These traits, in Blassingame's view, did not necessarily reflect the slaves' real personalities. It was simply that side of their personality they presented to whites. Some of the characteristics were masks - the aim of which was to mislead the owner. 'Ritual deference' to whites was natural enough behaviour when slaves could be punished for showing disrespect. Historians now generally accept that slaves showed as many character and behaviour traits as whites.

Genovese and Blassingame have both shown that slaves, far from being 'conditioned' by their white owners, were active participants in their own development. They did have their own 'domains' - or 'space', free from white interference. The slave family was a particularly vital unit. Despite the threat of forced sale, most slaves lived in two-parent family groups and slave marriages were surprisingly stable and long-lasting. (Many slave owners made notable efforts to keep slave families together.) The family, as Blassingame as pointed out, was a 'zone of safety'. By giving slaves love, individual identity and a sense of personal worth, it helped mitigate some of the severity of slavery. The realities of slavery, moreover, forced the creation of an extended family which helped protect children, in particular, if and when a family member was sold. Most slave children, therefore, had many aunts, uncles and cousins who might or might not be real kin but who were prepared to assume family roles should a child be orphaned by the workings of the slave trade.

The family, with its extended kinship networks, was one of the most powerful transmitters of slave culture. Slave music - a means of expression, communication and protest - permeated many aspects of slave life, as did dance. Black folktales also helped foster a sense of community. The folktales, usually involving animals, often taught survival strategies. Weak animals overcame more powerful and threatening opponents by using wit and guile. (Many of these stories have come down to us as 'Br'er Rabbit' tales.)

Religion, which played an important part in the life of many slaves, may also have been a vital cultural transmitter. Some historians think that the first African slaves brought many of their traditional beliefs, values and rituals with them to America and that these were grafted on to Christianity with the result that slaves evolved their own distinctive style of worship. Black churches and black ministers were not uncommon by the 1850s. However, other historians think that slaves, most of whom attended white churches before the Civil War (sitting in segregated pews), simply copied white Southern practices. The style of preaching and active congregational participation that became typical of black churches was typical of churches generally in the ante-bellum South. Indeed, it can be claimed that the Church was the most important institution for the Americanisation of the slaves: arguably in no other aspect of black cultural life did the values and practices of whites so deeply penetrate.

10 Was Slavery Profitable?

Economists and politicians in the mid-nineteenth century debated whether slavery was economically profitable. Historians have continued the debate. Much depends on defining just who slavery might have been profitable for. Was it profitable for the slave? Was it profitable for the slaveowners? Did it benefit the economy of the South as a whole? Much of the debate about the extent to which slaves benefited from slavery has already been outlined. Relatively few historians now claim that slavery was profitable for the slave. Fogel and Engermann's claim that slaves kept 90 per cent of their labour has been dismissed by most historians. Whether slavery was profitable for individual slaveowners is perhaps something of a red herring. Slaveowners obviously believed that it was profitable to buy slaves or it is unlikely they would have done so. No one doubts that slavery made a minority of white Southerners enormously wealthy. Slaveholding enabled planters to increase their cotton acreage and hence their profits. The rising price of slaves also strongly suggests that slaves were a good investment.

A far more interesting debate is the extent to which the economy of the South gained or lost by slavery. It is possible that slavery was a good business proposition for the slaveholder but a poor economic proposition for the South as a whole. This was certainly the view of most ante-bellum Northerners. In 1857 a Southerner, Hilton Rowan Helper published an influential book - *The Impending Crisis of the South* - in which he argued that slavery was responsible for the economic decline of the South. (The book, dedicated to the non-slaveholding Southern whites, displayed relatively little sympathy for slaves as such.) 'Slavery, and nothing but slavery', said Helper, 'has retarded the progress and prosperity of our portion of the Union; depopulated and impoverished our cities by forcing the more industrious and enterprising natives of the soil to emigrate to the free states; brought our domain under a sparse and inert population by preventing foreign immigration; made us tributary to the North, and reduced us to the humiliating condition of mere provincial subjects in fact, though not in name.'

In the twentieth century, a number of historians (e.g. Phillips) have followed Helper's line and seen slavery as a burden to the economic growth of the South. They have claimed that slavery did not fully utilise the potential skills of the labour force. Arguably it helped bring manual labour into disrepute among Southern whites, thus helping to undermine the work ethic, and did not help the economic well-being of the non-slaveholders who suffered from wage levels depressed by slave competition. Genovese has argued that most great planters were not particularly capitalist-inclined, a fact which may have retarded Southern economic growth. It is also possible to claim that slaves were a poor capital investment and that Southern capital would have been better spent on investment in manufacturing and transport.

Some historians have stressed the incompatibility between slavery and an urban, industrial society - a fact noted by some ante-bellum Southerners. Slaves in cities were much more difficult to supervise and were also exposed to all kinds of dangerous ideas about freedom. Slavery may thus have imposed a certain rigidity upon the Southern mind and upon the Southern economy, ensuring that the South opposed industrialisation and remained economically dependent on staple-crop agriculture - especially cotton. Cotton prices were subject to the vagaries of both the climate and international trade. It is true that cotton fetched good prices throughout the 1850s, which led to an increase in the

Sale of Slaves and Stock.

The Negroes and Stock listed below, are a Prime Lot, and belong to the ESTATE OF THE LATE LUTHER McGOWAN, and will be sold on Monday, Sept. 22nd, 1852, at the Fair Grounds, in Savannah, Georgia, at 1:00 P. M. The Negroes will be taken to the grounds two days previous to the Sale, so that they may be inspected by prospective buyers.

On account of the low prices listed below, they will be sold for cash only, and must be taken into custody within two hours after sale.

No.	Name	Age	Remarks.	Price.
1	Lunesta	27	Prime Rice Planter,	$1,275.00
2	Violet	16	Housework and Nursemaid,	900.00
3	Lizzie	30	Rice, Unsound,	300.00
4	Minda	27	Cotton, Prime Woman,	1,200.00
5	Adam	28	Cotton, Prime Young Man,	1,100.00
6	Abel	41	Rice Hand, Eyesight Poor,	675.00
7	Tanney	22	Prime Cotton Hand,	950.00
8	Flementina	39	Good Cook, Stiff Knee,	400.00
9	Lanney	34	Prime Cottom Man,	1,000.00
10	Sally	10	Handy in Kitchen,	675.00
11	Maccabey	35	Prime Man, Fair Carpenter,	980.00
12	Dorcas Judy	25	Seamstress, Handy in House,	800.00
13	Happy	60	Blacksmith,	575.00
14	Mowden	15	Prime Cotton Boy,	700.00
15	Bills	21	Handy with Mules,	900.00
16	Theopolis	39	Rice Hand, Gets Fits,	575.00
17	Coolidge	29	Rice Hand and Blacksmith,	1,275.00
18	Bessie	69	Infirm, Sews,	250.00
19	Infant	1	Strong Likely Boy	400.00
20	Samson	41	Prime Man, Good with Stock,	975.00
21	Callie May	27	Prime Woman, Rice,	1,000.00
22	Honey	14	Prime Girl, Hearing Poor,	850.00
23	Angelina	16	Prime Girl, House or Field,	1,000.00
24	Virgil	21	Prime Field Hand,	1,100.00
25	Tom	40	Rice Hand, Lame Leg,	750.00
26	Noble	11	Handy Boy,	900.00
27	Judge Lesh	55	Prime Blacksmith,	800.00
28	Booster	43	Fair Mason, Unsound,	600.00
29	Big Kate	37	Housekeeper and Nurse,	950.00
30	Melie Ann	19	Housework, Smart Yellow Girl,	1,250.00
31	Deacon	26	Prime Rice Hand,	1,000.00
32	Coming	19	Prime Cotton Hand,	1,000.00
33	Mabel	47	Prime Cotton Hand,	800.00
34	Uncle Tim	60	Fair Hand with Mules,	600.00
35	Abe	27	Prime Cotton Hand,	1,000.00
36	Tennes	29	Prime Rice Hand and Coachman,	1,250.00

There will also be offered at this sale, twenty head of Horses and Mules with harness, along with thirty head of Prime Cattle. Slaves will be sold separate, or in lots, as best suits the purchaser. Sale will be held rain or shine.

Notice of a slave sale, 1852

amount of cotton grown and rising slave prices. But some historians believe that the boom in cotton was almost over. Competition from other cotton-producing countries was bound to result in falling world prices. If the demand for cotton decreased - as it was to do after the Civil War - the Southern economy would be in tatters.

However, a clutch of recent historians - Stampp, Conrad and Meyer, and Fogel and Engerman - have argued (persuasively) that slavery was an efficient and vibrant form of economic organisation which did not deter the growth of the Southern economy. Cotton was certainly profitable in the mid-nineteenth century. Investment in slaves, therefore, was by no means a waste of capital. Moreover slave prices nearly doubled in the 1850s. Southern investors in slaves, therefore, received returns roughly equal to the returns of those Northerners who invested in manufacturing industry or railways. The fact that the South lagged behind the North in industrial development can be interpreted as testimony to the health - not the sickness - of the slave economy. The section was making so much money it had no incentive to industrialise.

From 1840 to 1860 the increase in per capita income in the South exceeded the rate of increase in the rest of the USA. This was largely due to cotton. The South faced no immediate threat to its world dominance. Southern plantations grew cotton more efficiently - and thus more cheaply - than any other area in the world. Fogel and Engermann and James Oakes have flatly contradicted Genovese's view that slaveowners were essentially paternalistic. They see them as shrewd businessmen, obsessed with their own personal economic advancement. Such was the pressure to succeed economically, that many Southerners (especially the younger sons of planters) left home and moved westwards in search of prosperity. Fogel and Engermann have gone further, arguing that Southern slave agriculture, as a result of specialisation, careful management and economies of scale, was 35 per cent more efficient than small-scale family farming in the North. This claim is not totally convincing; it is impossible to make a fair comparison between large-scale plantations producing cotton for export and a small Northern family farm, involved in mixed-farming: the two were different in scale, structure and purpose. However, it could be that Southern planters, as a whole, were more prepared to experiment with scientific agricultural techniques than Northern farmers.

Slavery was not just linked to cotton. Slave labour could be used in a variety of tasks in competition with white labour. It was even adaptable to an urban and industrial environment. Slaves were used successfully in factories such as the Tredegar Iron Works in Richmond and in coal mining. The fact that industry did not develop on any great scale in the South was simply because cotton production was so profitable. Most slaves, therefore, were put to work on plantations.

11 The Future of Slavery

Some historians have argued that once cotton prices fell - as surely they one day must - then slavery would have withered away and died of its own accord. If this is correct, the terrible blood-letting of the Civil War was unnecessary. However, there is little evidence to support such a view. Although slavery was declining in parts of the upper South on the eve of the Civil War, in most of the South it was flourishing as never before. Given the world-wide demand for cotton, there is no valid economic reason for believing slavery was about to die out. James Hammond of South Carolina was coldly realistic when he posed his rhetorical question: '[Were] ever any people, civilised or savage, persuaded by arguments, human or divine, to surrender voluntarily two billion dollars?'.

Moreover, slavery was not simply an economic institution. It was also a system of racial control. It kept the millions of blacks in the South in their place and ensured white supremacy. Even the poorest, non-slaveholding whites felt they had a vested interest in preserving slavery: it kept them off the bottom of the social heap. Poor whites were considered - and considered themselves - superior to slaves. Most Southerners feared that an end to slavery would result in economic collapse, social disintegration and race war. Thus slave-owners and non-slave-owners alike were committed to the South's own peculiar institution: so committed that (ultimately) they were prepared to secede from the Union and wage a terrible four year war in a (misplaced) effort to maintain it. Given the South's commitment to slavery, it is difficult to see how it would have withered away without the Civil War.

Making notes on 'The Peculiar Institution'

Your notes on this chapter should give you an understanding of some of the debates and controversies surrounding the peculiar institution. Many of these debates - continuations of debates which began in the United States before the Civil War - still have plenty of life left in them. Your notes should particularly focus on the following issues:

1   Why did slavery die out in the North but continue in the South?
2   Why did militant abolitionism develop in the North and what impact did it have?
3   Why and how did the South defend its peculiar institution?
4   How benign was slavery?
5   How did slavery in the USA compare with slavery elsewhere?
6   What impact did slavery have on slave personality and slave culture?
7   What impact did slavery have on the Southern economy?

Answering essay questions on 'The Peculiar Institution'

The following are potential questions on this topic:

1 Was there any truth in the Southern claim that slavery was both a benign and profitable institution in mid-nineteenth century America?
2 Account for the lack of slave rebellions in the ante-bellum South.

While much of the content of these essays is likely to be similar, the emphasis in each should be very different. Question 1 is really two questions in one: was slavery 'benign'; was it profitable? You might decide it was not benign but was profitable (as Kenneth Stampp argued) or not profitable but benign (as Ulrich Phillips claimed). You might also argue it was both benign and profitable or neither benign nor profitable! It is up to you to decide. But the important thing is that you have good evidence to support your case. It is also useful if you can show, along the way, that you are very much aware of views which differ from your own.

Question 2 is more difficult. You first need to know what slave 'rebellions' actually occurred. (Is the question correct in assuming there were few rebellions?) Assuming you know that there were only three conspiracies of major importance (and two of these never got beyond the planning stage), you then have to explain why there was no mass slave revolt. Draw up a rough plan for this question. What would you be saying in your introduction? How many paragraphs do you envisage writing (7 or 8 is usually about right) and what would be the emphasis of each paragraph? Write down your actual conclusion - and remember to answer the question. Why were there so few rebellions?

Source-based questions on 'The Peculiar Institution'

1 The Notice of a Slave Sale
Examine the Slave Sale Notice on page 42. Answer the following questions:
a) How useful is this source for historians studying the nature of the peculiar institution? (6 marks)
b) Comment on the slave prices. (5 marks)
c) Comment on the fact that the slaves were to be sold 'separate or in lots'. (4 marks)
d) Comment on the type and range of work done by the slaves of Luther McGowan. (5 marks)
e) What does the source tell us about Luther McGowan? (5 marks)

2 The Slave Population
Examine the statistics on page 32. Answer the following questions:

a) To what extent is this statistical information likely to be accurate? (4 marks)
b) Which three states were most likely to be committed to defending slavery? Which three states were least likely to be committed to defending it? Explain your answer. (3 marks)
c) Comment on the number of Southern free blacks. (4 marks)
d) What does the statistical information NOT tell us about slave distribution? (4 marks)

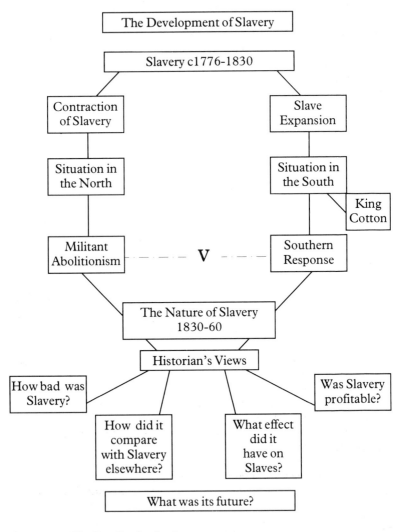

The Development of Slavery

Slavery c1776-1830

Contraction of Slavery

Slave Expansion

Situation in the North

Situation in the South

King Cotton

Militant Abolitionism — V — Southern Response

The Nature of Slavery 1830-60

Historian's Views

How bad was Slavery?

Was Slavery profitable?

How did it compare with Slavery elsewhere?

What effect did it have on Slaves?

What was its future?

Summary - The Peculiar Institution

CHAPTER 4

The Impact of the Mexican War

1 Introduction

In the early 1840s the second party system seemed responsive to most voters' needs. Most voters viewed themselves as Democrats or Whigs and developed strong attachments to their party. The struggle between the two national parties helped the United States avoid the latent sectional divisions within the country. However, events in the 1840s were to undermine both the second party system and sectional harmony. In 1846 the country went to war with Mexico. This war was to be one of the most successful wars in the history of the United States. At a relatively small cost in terms of American lives, the USA won a colossal area of Mexican territory. However, acquisition of this territory was to result in a series of crises which set Southerners against Northerners and which threatened to tear the Union apart.

2 The Problem of Western Expansion

Western expansion had been a problem for the USA from the early nineteenth century. Slavery underpinned that problem. As the continent was settled and new states applied to join the Union, there was one crucial question in the minds of most Americans: would the new state be free or slave? The first serious crisis occurred in 1819. By this stage the original 13 states had grown to 22. 11 of these states were free: 11 were slave states. In 1819 Missouri applied to join the Union as a slave state. Given that this would tilt the balance against them, Northern states opposed Missouri's admittance. The result was a series of furious debates with Southern Congressmen lined up solidly against Northern Congressmen. In the end, the politicians managed to reach agreement. To balance the admittance of Missouri, a new state of Maine was carved out of Massachusetts and admitted to the Union as a free state. It was also agreed that henceforward, there should be no slavery in the Louisiana Purchase Territory, north of latitude 36° 30. South of that line, slavery could exist. This 'Missouri Compromise' proved satisfactory to both North and South and tension eased. Nevertheless the issues raised in 1819-20 frightened many of America's elder statesmen. 'This momentous question, like a fire bell in the night, awakened and filled me with terror', declared former President Thomas Jefferson.

The next Western problem came in Texas in 1836. Americans had been encouraged to settle in Texas in the 1820s. Most of the settlers were Southerners and many had taken their slaves with them. In 1829 Mexico emancipated its slaves and the following year prohibited further American immigration into Texas. The American Texans defied both laws and for some years the Mexican government was too weak to enforce its authority. By 1835 there were about 30,000 American immigrants in Texas (plus 5,000 black slaves) and only about 5,000 Mexicans. The efforts of the new Mexican leader, General Santa Anna, to enforce Mexican authority were resented by the American Texans and over the winter of 1835-6 they declared independence. Santa Anna quickly marched north with a large Mexican army. A small Texas force of 187 men put up a spirited defence of the Alamo, a fortified mission, but this fell in early March 1836. All the Texan defenders, including the western heroes Jim Bowie and Davy Crockett, were killed. Two weeks later the Mexicans captured Goliad, massacring over 300 Texans. Although President Andrew Jackson sympathised with the Texans' struggle for independence, he sent no official help. However, hundreds of Americans from the South and West rushed to the aid of the Texans and in April 1836 an American-Texan army, led by Sam Houston, defeated the Mexicans at the battle of San Jacinto. Santa Anna was captured and forced to recognise the independence of Texas.

Although the Mexican government never officially ratified Santa Anna's action, Texas was now effectively independent. Most Texans hoped to join the United States, a move which most Southerners supported. However, many Northerners were opposed to immediate annexation. Some were concerned that such action might spark war with Mexico. But more important was the fear that the acquisition of Texas would lead to the spread of slavery and strengthen Southern political power. So large was Texas that it might well be divided into five new slave states, which would obviously tilt the balance between free and slave states heavily in the South's favour. Some Northerners thought the Texas rebellion was all part of a 'Slave Power' conspiracy - a criminal act sparked by slaveowners. Given that Texas was obviously a political hot potato and that 1836 was a presidential election year, Jackson shelved the issue. So too did his successor Martin Van Buren. The result was that for a few years Texas was an independent - Lone Star - republic, unrecognised by Mexico and rejected by the USA.

But from 1836 onwards there was continued agitation for annexation both from the Texans and from American nationalists, particularly Southerners and Westerners. Northerners, for the most part, continued to oppose annexation and were not even particularly impressed by the rumour (spread by Texans and nationalists) that Britain had designs on Texas. Most politicians, aware that the annexation of Texas might open a Pandora's box of - sectional - troubles, tried to avoid the issue. However, the issue of Texas - and Western expansion generally - would not go away and became a major issue in the 1844 presidential election, fought between the Whig Henry Clay (who opposed the annexation of Texas) and the Democrat James Polk. During the election, Polk, a slaveholder from Tennessee, committed himself to both the annexation of Texas and the whole of Oregon - an area in dispute with Britain. This expansionist programme proved popular and Polk was elected President. The outgoing (Southern) Whig President Tyler, anxious to leave his mark on events, now secured a joint resolution of Congress in favour of annexation of Texas. This was signed by Tyler in his last days in office in March 1845. In July 1845 Texas accepted the US terms and was finally admitted into the Union, as a single state, in December 1845. Mexico immediately severed diplomatic relations with the USA.

Polk, committed to Western expansion, was anxious to annex California and New Mexico, provinces over which Mexico exerted little control. (The Mexican population was small and scattered and a few Americans were already beginning to settle in both areas.) Many Americans supported the President. In 1845 a Democrat journalist, John O'Sullivan, declared, 'it is our manifest destiny to overspread and to possess the whole of the continent which Providence has given us for the development of the great experiment of liberty and federated self-government entrusted to us'. Advocates of 'manifest destiny' - usually Democrats - invariably invoked God, nature and the glory of republican institutions, to sanction expansion. Northern Whigs tended to be more cynical. Many saw the lofty rhetoric as a smoke screen aimed at concealing the evil intent of expanding slavery.

3 'Mr Polk's War': 1846-8

The USA's annexation of Texas angered Mexico, which still claimed sovereignty over the Lone Star state. The fact that there were disputed boundaries between Texas and Mexico was a further problem. There were other difficulties. One long-standing United States' grievance was the failure of the Mexican government to pay some $2 million in debts it owed to American citizens, largely for damage to property destroyed in recurrent periods of disorder in Mexico. The barely concealed United States designs on California and New Mexico did not help US-Mexican relations which deteriorated rapidly in 1845-6. Efforts to reach some kind of negotiated agreement were hindered by the fact that the internal situation in Mexico was volatile. Mexican governments came and went with such rapidity that it was difficult for the United States to know with whom to deal. Polk hoped to persuade Mexico to sell the territory he coveted and in November 1845 sent John Slidell as his special emissary to Mexico with the authority to offer $30 million for New Mexico and California. Unfortunately, Slidell arrived in Mexico City at a time when a new government had just come to power on a tide of anti-Americanism. This government refused to have anything to do with him.

Polk now sent American troops, led by General Zachary Taylor, into the disputed Texas-Mexican area north of the Rio Grande river. His intention was clear: he hoped to provoke an incident that would result in war - a war which would lead to American annexation of California and New Mexico. But Polk's action did not immediately provoke a Mexican response. In May 1846, his patience at an end, Polk decided to ask Congress for a declaration of war on the grounds that Mexico refused to pay its debts to the USA and also insulted the country by declining to negotiate with the Slidell mission. That same evening, just before the war message was made public, news arrived that Mexican troops had crossed the Rio Grande, and ambushed a party of American troops, killing or wounding 16 men. This was the pretext Polk had been waiting for. Hastily revising his war message and bending the facts to suit his purpose, he declared that Mexicans had 'shed American blood on American soil'. War, he stated, 'exists by the act of Mexico herself' and he asked Congress to acknowledge the fact and vote money to fight the war. There was some opposition, particularly from Northern Whigs who pointed out that the Mexican attack had occurred in an area that no previous administration had claimed as part of the USA. Nevertheless, Congress accepted Polk's version of events and voted overwhelmingly for war.

While most Southerners and Westerners fully supported the war, many Northerners remained cynical. They saw the Mexican War as a Southern war of aggression which had been incited, they suspected, by Polk: indeed the war was known in the North as 'Mr Polk's War'. However, Mexican leaders, who showed no willingness to reach any agreement, certainly deserve some of the blame for the war. Aware that their army was four times the size of the USA regular army, many Mexicans were confident of victory if war came.

From Mexico's point of view, however, the war was to be a disaster. Although the USA had a smaller army, it had twice as many people and a much stronger industrial base than Mexico and thus far greater military potential. The Mexican armies were poorly led, badly organised and poorly equipped. The USA's main advantages were its superior artillery, its pool of about 700 junior officers, most of whom had been efficiently trained at West Point, its enthusiastic (mainly Southern and Western) volunteers, and the fact that it controlled the sea.

The war began with United States forces quickly occupying California and New Mexico. In the summer of 1846 US cavalry, led by Colonel Kearney, marched unopposed into Santa Fé and proclaimed the annexation of New Mexico. Kearney then set off on the long march to California. By the time he arrived the province was largely under United States control. In May 1846 American settlers in California had proclaimed independence from Mexico. They were soon helped by Colonel John Frémont, in the region on an exploratory expedition, and by an American naval detachment conveniently stationed off the California coast. Kearney's arrival in California in December, ended what little Mexican resistance remained. Polk hoped that the Mexicans would recognise the inevitable and accept the loss of New Mexico and California. But a new Mexican government, led by none other than General Santa Anna, refused to surrender and the war continued.

The American war heroes were General Zachary Taylor and General

Winfield Scott. Taylor won a series of victories over Santa Anna in Northern Mexico in 1846 and then, despite being outnumbered by four to one, defeated the Mexicans at the battle of Buena Vista in February 1847. Polk, meanwhile, had decided to strike at Mexico City. General Scott captured Vera Cruz in February 1847. Then, with under 11,000 men and facing determined Mexican resistance, Scott marched 260 miles inland over difficult terrain, storming several fortresses before finally capturing Mexico City in September 1847.

By the autumn of 1847 the Mexican War was essentially over. It had cost the Americans $100 million and 13,000 dead soldiers. (2,000 died in battle: 11,000 died of disease.) The USA was now in a position to enforce peace. Some Southerners called for the annexation of 'All Mexico' - a view with which Polk had some sympathy. However, many Northerners wanted to annex no territory whatsoever. Peace-making was further complicated by the fact that there was no obvious government in Mexico with which to deal. In the event, Polk's envoy Nicholas Trist eventually negotiated a peace treaty with a Mexican government largely 'created' by the Americans. Trist, although basing his negotiations on his original instructions, acted very much on his own initiative. Indeed, he had been officially recalled by Polk a few days before the treaty was agreed!

By the Treaty of Guadalupe Hidalgo, signed in February 1848, California and New Mexico (including present day Nevada, Utah, most of Arizona, and parts of Colorado and Wyoming) were ceded to the USA. In return for this huge area - 500,000 square miles, over one third of Mexico's national territory and two fifths of the USA's present territory - the American government agreed to pay Mexico $15,000,000 and to assume the claims of American citizens against Mexico, amounting to some $3,250,000. Polk, incensed at Trist's disobedience, was unhappy with the Treaty. Despite the fact that the USA had gained everything it had gone to war for, he thought even more territory could have been gained. Spurred on by Southern firebrands - who saw the dizzy prospect of dozens of new slave states - Polk considered rejecting the Treaty. But given Northern opinion and the fact that some Southerners balked at the notion of ruling Mexico's large mixed Spanish and Indian population, Polk reluctantly accepted the Treaty , which was ratified by the Senate by 38 votes to 14 in May 1848.

4 The Wilmot Proviso, 1846

The Mexican War, which was fully reported in American newspapers, gripped the popular imagination and fuelled soaring nationalism in many parts of the United States. However, the war also revived controversy over the extension of slavery and ushered in a period of sectional strife that was not to end until the Civil War.

Americans had anticipated winning territory from the start of the war.

Many politicians had been worried at the consequences because it was unclear whether states created from the land won from Mexico would ultimately become slave or free. In August 1846 David Wilmot, a Northern Democrat from Pennsylvania, added an amendment to an appropriations (finance) bill in the House of Representatives. By the so-called Wilmot Proviso, slavery was to be excluded from any territory gained from Mexico as a result of the war.

Wilmot was not an abolitionist. Nor were most of the Northern Democrats who supported his Proviso. Like Wilmot himself, they had a number of motives. Perhaps chief amongst these was the fact that many resented Southern control of their party. Polk surrounded himself with Southerners. While happy to fight the Mexican War (in the apparent interest of the Slave Power), the President had reneged on his promise to take the whole of Oregon. Instead an agreement had been reached whereby Britain took the area north of the 49th parallel: the United States was to have southern Oregon. This treaty, signed in 1846, made considerable sense: the United States did quite well out of the deal; and it would have been foolish for Polk to have fought Mexico and Britain at one and the same time. But Northern Democrats felt that Polk's appeasement of Britain, coupled with his forceful action against Mexico, symbolised his pro-Southern bias. Northern Democrats, especially those in Pennsylvania, also had economic grievances. In 1846 Southern Democrats, with Polk's backing, had supported an act lowering tariffs: this at a time when most Pennsylvanians wanted a higher, protective tariff. Furthermore, North-western Democrats resented the fact that Polk had vetoed two bills providing Federal funds for improvement of navigation on the western rivers.

Wilmot and most Northern Democrats had little humanitarian concern for slaves. In supporting the Wilmot Proviso, their main concern was simply to keep blacks out of the Mexican territories and ensure the land was settled by free whites, who would not face competition from large-scale plantations dependent on slave labour. In Wilmot's own words, his Proviso aimed to preserve the ex-Mexican territories for 'the sons of toil, of my own race and own colour'. Concerned at the coming mid-term elections, Northern Democrats were warning Polk of their unease with the direction of his policies. Interestingly, it was Northern Democrats, in the late 1840s, who talked of the threat of the 'Slave Power'.

Polk was not impressed. He denounced the Proviso as 'mischievous and foolish'. Most Southern Congressmen - Democrats and Whigs alike - were similarly outraged at Wilmot's proposal. After a bitter debate, the Proviso passed the House of Representatives by 83 votes to 64. The voting was strictly sectional: every Southern Democrat and all but two Southern Whigs voted against it. Most Northerners voted for it. The Proviso, however, failed to pass the Senate and thus did not become law. But the matter did not end there. For anti-slavery forces, the Proviso became a rallying cry. Many Northern state legislatures endorsed it. Most Southern states, on the other hand, believing that slavery had to expand to survive, denounced it. Senator Robert Toombs of Georgia warned that if Congress passed the Proviso, he would favour disunion rather than 'degradation'.

5 The Calhoun Doctrine

Northerners believed that Congress had the power to exclude slavery from the territories and should exercise that power. But Southerners responded aggressively to the Northern threat and for the first time challenged the doctrine of Congressional authority to regulate or prohibit slavery in the territories. John Calhoun from South Carolina, played a crucial role. Calhoun had first entered Congress in 1811. He had then been an out-and-out American nationalist, supporting increasing Federal power at the expense of state rights. However, in the late 1820s he changed his mind and developed the doctrine of nullification. This had proclaimed the right of any state to overrule or modify any Federal law deemed unconstitutional. The crisis over nullification came to a head in 1832-3 when South Carolina disallowed two Federal tariff acts. President Jackson labelled this action treason and threatened to use force. South Carolina, unable to muster support from other Southern states, pulled back from declaring secession and Jackson, in return, lowered tariffs.

Calhoun remained a force to be reckoned with. In February 1847 he issued a series of resolutions, subsequently known as 'The Platform of the South'. Asserting that the territories were common property of all the states, Calhoun claimed that citizens from every state had the right to migrate to any territory and to take their property (including slaves) with them. Congress, asserted Calhoun, had no constitutional authority to place restrictions on slavery in the territories and that the majority in the North were riding rough-shod over the rights of the Southern minority. If this continued, the Southern states would have little option but to secede and would be justified in so doing. All the states, in Calhoun's view, were sovereign states. They had not sacrificed their sovereignty when they ratified the 1787 Constitution.

6 The Search for Compromise

The 30th Congress met in December 1847. The Senate, in the view of the historian Alan Nevins, contained 'a galaxy of talent which had lifted it to a prestige perhaps never since equalled'. Talent was most definitely needed. The problem of slavery expansion divided Northerners from Southerners, preoccupied Congress to the exclusion of every other issue, and threatened to destroy the unity of the main political parties.

A compromise of some sort seemed essential. The preferred solution of some, including (eventually) President Polk, was simply to continue the 36° 30 line across the Continent. Slavery would be banned in any territory gained from Mexico north of this line but would be allowed south of the line. This proposal did not appeal to Northerners who wished to see no further slavery expansion or Southerners who wished to see slavery expand anywhere. This solution, therefore, was voted down in the House.

A far more successful compromise idea was the notion of 'squatter' or popular sovereignty. This was particularly associated with two Mid-western Democrat politicians, Senator Lewis Cass of Michigan and Senator Stephen Douglas of Illinois. They held that it was not Congress which should decide on whether a territory should or should not allow slaves. Instead, the decision should be made by the people in the territory. This solution was obviously consistent with democracy and self-government. Moreover, it seemed to offer something to both sections. It met the South's wish for Federal non-intervention and held out the prospect that slavery might be extended to some of the Mexican territories. But it could also be plausibly presented to the North as an exclusion scheme because it was unlikely that most of the settlers in the new territories would actually vote for the introduction of slavery.

However, there were problems with the concept of popular sovereignty. First, it went against previous practice. In the past, Congress had decided on what should happen in the territories. Did popular sovereignty mean that it no longer had that power? There were also serious practical difficulties. The main problem was when exactly a territory should decide on the slavery question. Northern Democrats (including both Cass and Douglas) envisaged that the decision should be taken early - as soon as the first territorial assembly met. Southern Democrats, however, keen to ensure that slaves were allowed into territories, saw the decision being made late - near the end of the territorial phase when settlers were involved in drafting a state constitution and seeking admission to the Union. In the interim, they envisaged that slavery would be recognised and protected. Despite this ambiguity, and despite the fact that it was defended in different ways by Northerners and Southerners, popular sovereignty was supported by many Democrats. It was opposed by some Southerners who thought they had the right to take their 'property' anywhere they wanted and by Northern abolitionists who believed that slavery should not be allowed to expand under any circumstances, not even if the majority of white settlers wished it to expand.

7 The 1848 Election

Although Polk had presided over an administration which had won the greatest area of territory in United States history, he gained little personal credit for the Mexican War, and, worn out by constant opposition, pledged not to seek a second term. The Democrat party thus had to choose a successor. Some Southerners wanted to nominate Calhoun. Northerners, on the other hand, favoured ex-President Martin Van Buren of New York. The nomination of either of these men would have split the Democrats in two. The party, therefore, rallied around a 'safe' compromise candidate - Lewis Cass of Michigan. Cass and the Democrats supported popular sovereignty and praised Polk's expansionist policies. However, the Democrats ran two very different campaigns. In the South, they emphasised Cass's pledge to veto the Wilmot Proviso should Congress ever pass it. In the North, they argued, if pressed, that popular sovereignty would result in free soil as surely as a Congressional prohibition - without threatening the bonds of union.

The Whig party nominated the Mexican war hero Zachary Taylor. Taylor, had no previous political experience and had never before even voted in a presidential election. Many leading Whigs were not altogether sure he was a Whig! The fact that he was also a Louisiana slaveowner did not endear him to Northern abolitionists. Nevertheless, many Northern Whigs were prepared to endorse Taylor if only because he seemed a likely winner. To avoid a major split between its Northern and Southern wings, the Whig party had no national platform on slavery expansion. This meant that, like the Democrats, it could conduct a two-faced campaign, running as a free soil, pro-Proviso party in the North and as an anti-Proviso, pro-Southern rights party in the South.

A new party was also formed to fight the election. This was the Free Soil Party. It included a number of Northern Democrats, especially the 'Barnburners' from New York state who supported Van Buren, disliked Cass, and were alarmed at the increasing Southern dominance of the Democrat party. (The 'Barnburners' got their name because they were said to resemble the farmer who was willing to burn down his barn in order to get rid of rats!) The new party also included 'Conscience' Whigs who had no intention of campaigning for a Southern slaveowner. Finally, the party incorporated the - abolitionist - Liberty party which had won less than 3 per cent of the vote in 1844. Van Buren was nominated as the Free Soil party's presidential candidate. The party supported the Wilmot Proviso and promised: 'Free soil, free speech, free labour, free men'.

The election was a triumph for Taylor who won 1,360,000 votes (47.5 per cent of the total) and 163 electoral college votes. Cass only won 1,220,000 votes (42.5 per cent) and 127 electoral college votes. Van Buren won a respectable 291,000 votes (10 per cent) but failed to carry a single state and thus won no electoral college votes. Taylor's victory was not sectional. He carried 8 of the 15 slave states and 7 of the 15 free states. Nevertheless, sectional issues most certainly influenced the election. Throughout the election, the expansion of slavery had been the crucial issue. The fact that the Free Soil party won 10 per cent of the popular vote was some indication of Northern opinion. Van Buren drew so heavily on Democrat support in New York that he effectively gave the state - and the election - to Taylor.

The Congress, which met in December 1848, continued to be dominated by debates over slavery. Northern representatives, who controlled the House, reaffirmed the Wilmot Proviso and condemned the slave trade in the District of Columbia. Sectional antagonism was the order of the day. The same month that Congress met Calhoun issued his 'Address to the People of the Southern States' - an effort to unite all Southern Congressmen behind the 'Southern cause'. The 'Address' was very much a defence of slavery and an attack on Northern aggression. Calhoun's tactic, however, failed. At this stage, most Southern Whigs placed their trust in President Taylor and were not prepared to support Calhoun. Only about one third of slave state members of Congress were prepared to sign Calhoun's 'Address'.

Events in California led to further animosity. Few Americans had thought that California (or New Mexico) would speedily apply for statehood if only because both areas seemed to have little to offer to settlers. But in January 1848, gold was discovered in the Sacramento Valley. This touched off the 1848-9 Gold Rush. The 'forty-niners' poured into California from all over the world. Some travelled overland by covered wagon: others took sailing ships round Cape Horn; some took the short cut across the isthmus of Panama. Within months, there were 100,000 people in California - more than enough to enable the area to apply for statehood. California certainly needed territorial government, if only to deal with the massive problems of law and order associated with the huge influx of settlers.

New Mexico had fewer settlers. But thousands of Mormons had settled around Salt Lake City in 1846. They had hoped to establish their own state of Deseret. Now, as a result of the Mexican War, they found themselves under American jurisdiction. In the spring of 1849, the non-slave-holding - but polygamous - Mormons drew up a constitution and sought admission to the Union. This was an additional problem. The key problem was whether California - and New Mexico - would be allowed to have slavery, given that slavery had been illegal in both Mexican-owned areas before 1848.

8 President Taylor

Zachary Taylor, the new President, was (and is) generally seen as a man of honesty and integrity. But in political terms, he was judged by many contemporaries (and has been similarly judged by historians), as a stubborn, naive, political amateur who was prone to over-simplify complex problems. Although he was a Southern slave-owner, he was determined to act in a way that benefited the national interest as a whole. Surprisingly, and perhaps foolishly, Taylor deliberately shunned the

advice of Henry Clay of Kentucky and Daniel Webster of Massachusetts, the great Whig elder-statesmen. He was far more influenced by the
radical New York Senator William Seward, who was soon regarded as
the power behind the throne. Few Southern Whigs were happy with
Seward's prominence.

Congress's sitting came to an end in March 1849. It would not meet
again until December 1849. President Taylor, therefore, had to deal
with the problems of California and New Mexico. He determined to act
decisively. A quick solution to the problem might reduce the potential
for sectional strife. Taylor, who was opposed to the extension of slavery,
decided to encourage settlers in both California and New Mexico to
frame constitutions and apply immediately for admission to the Union -
without first going through the process of establishing territorial
governments. He was confident that people in both states would vote for
free state constitutions. This would obviously satisfy Northerners:
indeed in August 1849 he assured Northerners that they 'need have no
apprehension of the further extension of slavery'. Taylor was by no
means an abolitionist: he accepted the South's wish to defend slavery.
But he believed that slavery would be best protected if Southerners
refrained from rekindling the slavery issue in the territories. At the same
time, he hoped his policy would acknowledge a position upon which all
Southerners agreed: that is, that a state could bar or permit slavery as it
chose.

Taylor's policy quickly became reality. In the autumn of 1849
California drafted and ratified a constitution prohibiting slavery and
applied for immediate admission to the Union. It seemed that Taylor
was also prepared to admit New Mexico, even though it had not enough
people to apply for statehood. There was a further problem with New
Mexico: it had a major boundary dispute with Texas. Most Southerners
supported Texas's claim: most Northerners - and President Taylor -
supported New Mexico. A clash between the state forces of Texas and
the United States army suddenly seemed imminent.

9 Southern Resentment

Taylor miscalculated the anger his actions caused in the South,
especially among Southern Whigs who felt that the President had
betrayed them. Most Southerners, believed that having won the war
against Mexico, they were now being excluded from the territory gained.
Many appreciated that the climate and terrain of the area made it
inhospitable to slavery: there was no great rush to take slaves into New
Mexico or California. Nevertheless, most Southerners believed they
should have the right to expand. If a Northern majority could bar slavery
from common territory, Southerner citizens claimed they were no longer
equals of Northern citizens. Southerners - Democrats and Whigs alike -
accused Taylor of pressing California into applying for statehood before

its citizens really wanted it and without going through the proper procedures. Virtually all Southerners agreed that California and New Mexico should not be admitted to the Union without substantial compensation to the South. Some Southerners went further. 'If the scheme excluding slavery from California and New Mexico should be carried out - if we are to be reduced to a mere handful...woe, woe, I say to this Union', declared Calhoun. In October 1849 Mississippi issued a call to all slave states to send representatives to a convention to meet at Nashville (Tennessee) in June 1850. The convention would aim to devise and adopt 'some mode of resistance to Northern aggression'.

Taylor's hopes of resolving the sectional strife were dashed. Bitter sectional divisions were reflected in the 31st Congress which met in December 1849. The debates over slavery expansion were particularly fierce and fist fights on the floor of Congress became common place. Southerners also raised the issue of fugitive slaves, claiming (rightly) that many Northern states were flouting the (1793) law and actively frustrating slaveholders' efforts to catch runaways on northern soil and return them to the South. Northerners, on the other hand, objected to the fact that slavery - and the slave trade - were still allowed in the District of Columbia (i.e. in Washington). The dispute between Texas and New Mexico added to the tension - and more and more Southerners began to talk of secession.

10 The 1850 Compromise

President Taylor was determined to make no concessions to the South. Talk of secession did not worry him. He was prepared to call (what he saw as) the Southern bluff and, if need be, ready to lead an army into the South to enforce the laws and hang traitors. However, some Northern politicians were worried by events and felt that the South had to be placated. Most of the appeasers came from Mid-west states like Illinois or border states like Kentucky. Their leader was Henry Clay. Now 73 years old, Clay had served in Congress since 1812 and had come close to winning the presidency in 1844. Clay sympathised with slaveowners (he was one himself) but hated slavery! With a foot in both camps - and with a reputation as a conciliator from previous sectional crises - he seemed the ideal man to lead compromise efforts. His main problem was that, although a Whig, he had no standing with Taylor.

In January 1850 Clay offered the Senate a set of resolutions as a basis for a solution to the crisis. Some of the measures were designed to please the North: others the South. California was to be admitted as a free state. Utah (formerly the Mormon 'state' of Deseret) and New Mexico, on the other hand, were to be organised as territories without any mention of - or restriction on - slavery. Slave-trading but not slavery itself should end in the District of Columbia. A more stringent Fugitive Slave Act should be passed to placate the South. The Texas-New

Mexico dispute should also be settled. Texas should surrender the disputed land to New Mexico. In return Congress would assume the $10 million public debt which Texas still owed.

Clay rolled all of these proposals into a single 'omnibus' bill. The next seven months were to be marked by a series of epic speeches as Clay's Compromise proposals were discussed in Congress. Most of the 'old guard' politicians - many making their last major appearance on the public stage - contributed to the debates. So too did a number of men who were just beginning what were to be prestigious political careers. Clay defended his compromise proposals in a four-hour speech spread over two days in February 1850. The Senate galleries were packed. Copies of Clay's speech were in such demand that over 100,000 were printed. This is an extract:

1 I have seen many periods of great anxiety, of peril, and of danger in this country, and I have never before risen to address any assemblage so oppressed, so appalled, and so anxious; and sir, I hope it will not be out of place to do here what again and again I
5 have done in my private chamber, to implore of Him who holds the destinies of nations and individuals in His hands, to bestow upon our country His blessing, to calm the violence and rage of party, to still passion, to allow reason once more to resume its empire ... We are told now, and it is rung throughout this entire country, that the
10 Union is threatened with subversion and destruction. Well, the first question which naturally rises is, supposing the Union to be dissolved, - having all the causes of grievance which are complained of, - how far will a dissolution furnish a remedy for those grievances? If the Union is to be dissolved for any existing
15 causes, it will be dissolved because slavery is threatened to be abolished in the District of Columbia and because fugitive slaves are not returned, as in my opinion they ought to be ... Mr President, I am directly opposed to any purpose of secession, of separation. I am for staying within the Union, and defying any
20 portion of this Union to expel or drive me out of the Union.

Clay went on to warn the South against the evils of secession and assured the North that nature would check the spread of slavery more effectively than a thousand Wilmot Provisos.

Calhoun would have spoken but he was seriously ill. His speech, in consequence, was read by Senator James Mason of Virginia on 4 March. (Within a month of the speech Calhoun was dead.) The speech summarised what Calhoun had been saying for years. This is an extract:

1 What has caused this widely diffused and almost universal discontent? ... One of the causes is, undoubtedly, to be traced to

the long-continued agitation of the slave question on the part of the
North, and the many aggressions which they have made on the
5 rights of the South ... There is another lying back of it - with which
this is intimately connected - that may be regarded as the great and
primary cause. This is to be found in the fact that the equilibrium
between the two sections, in the Government as it stood when the
constitution was ratified and the Government put in action, has
10 been destroyed. At that time, there was nearly a perfect
equilibrium between the two ... but as it now stands, one section
has the exclusive power of controlling the Government, which
leaves the other without any adequate means of protecting itself
against its encroachments and oppression ... But if there was no
15 question of vital importance to the South, in reference to which
there was a diversity of views between the two sections, this state of
things might be endured, without the hazard of destruction to the
South. But such is not the fact. There is a question of vital
importance to the Southern section, in reference to which the
20 views and feelings of the two sections are as opposite and hostile as
they can possibly be. I refer to the relation between the two races in
the Southern section, which constitutes a vital portion of her social
organisation. Every portion of the North entertains views and
feelings more or less hostile to it ... On the contrary, the Southern
25 section regards the relation as one which cannot be destroyed
without subjecting the two races to the greatest calamity, and the
section to poverty, desolation, and wretchedness; and accordingly
they feel bound, by every consideration of interest and safety to
defend it ... How can the Union be saved? To this I answer, there is
30 but one way by which it can be - and that is - by adopting such
measures as will satisfy the States belonging to the Southern
section, that they can remain in the Union consistently with their
honour and their safety ... But can this be done? Yes, easily; not by
the weaker party, for it can of itself do nothing - not even protect
35 itself - but by the stronger. The North has only to will it to
accomplish it - to do justice by conceding to the South an equal
right in the acquired territory, and to do her duty by causing the
stipulations relative to fugitive slaves to be faithfully fulfilled - to
cease the agitation of the slave question.

On 7 March 1850 the 69 year old Daniel Webster, a Northern Whig
from Massachusetts, spoke in support of the Compromise.

1 I wish to speak today, not as a Massachusetts man, not as a
Northern man, but as an American and a member of the Senate of
the United States ... It is not to be denied that we live in the midst
of strong agitations and are surrounded by very considerable
5 dangers to our institutions and government ... I speak today for the

preservation of the Union ... I shall bestow a little attention, Sir,
upon these various grievances existing on the one side and on the
other. I begin with complaints of the South ... and especially to one
which has in my opinion just foundation; and that is, that there has
10 been found at the North, among individuals and among legislators,
a disinclination to perform fully their constitutional duties in
regard to the return of persons bound to service who have escaped
into the free states. In that respect, the South, in my judgement, is
right, and the North is wrong. Every member of every Northern
15 legislature is bound by oath ... to support the Constitution of the
United States; and the article of the Constitution which says to
these States they shall deliver up fugitives from service is as binding
in honour and conscience as any other article ... Peaceable
secession! ... Why, what would be the result? Where is the line to
20 be drawn? What states are to secede? What is to remain American?
What am I to be? An American no longer? Am I to become a
sectional man, a local man, a separatist with no country in
common with the gentlemen who sit around me here ... Heaven
forbid!

Webster, aware that his speech would offend many of his constituents,
aimed to offer an olive branch to the South. According to Alan Nevins,
'No speech more patriotic or evincing a higher degree of moral courage
had ever been made in Congress'. Moderates praised Webster's
devotion to the Union. But abolitionists bitterly denounced him for
betraying the cause of freedom.
    Among the 'new' men contributing to the debate were Stephen
Douglas, who defended the Compromise, and William Seward, who
condemned it as 'radically wrong and essentially vicious'. However
eloquent, the conciliatory voices of Clay, Webster and Douglas, they
made few converts. With every call for compromise, some Northern or
Southern speaker would rise and inflame passions. President Taylor soon
made it clear that he opposed Clay's Compromise proposals and would
not retreat from his position. In his view, California should be admitted as
a free state immediately while New Mexico should also come in with all
possible speed. Southerners would have to accept their medicine.
    In June 1850 delegates from nine of the fifteen slave states met at
Nashville. The fact that six slave states did not send delegates was
disconcerting to those 'fire-eaters' who supported secession. Even more
worrying was the fact that the Nashville convention displayed little
enthusiasm for secession. Moderates quickly took control of the
convention and isolated the extremists. It was clear that Southern
politicians were far from united. Southern Whigs were still hopeful that
some compromise could be arranged. The Nashville convention,
therefore, had little impact.
    President Taylor's death (of gastro-entiritus) on 9 July 1850, had a far

greater impact. Some contemporaries thought his death was timely. Daniel Webster was not alone in believing there would have been a Civil War if Taylor had lived. Taylor's Vice President Millard Fillmore now became President. A New York Whig, Fillmore was nevertheless sympathetic to the South and opposed to Seward. His break with the policies of his predecessor was immediately apparent. There were wholesale cabinet changes (Daniel Webster, for example, now became Secretary of State) and Fillmore immediately threw his weight behind the Compromise proposals. This did not have an immediate impact. On 31 July Clay's Omnibus Bill was defeated. The main reason for the defeat was the fact that many Northern Senators, anxious to escape the imputation of bargaining with the Slave Power, voted against it.

However, Clay's Compromise proposals were far from dead. Senator Douglas of Illinois now demonstrated his political skill. Known as the 'Little Giant' (he was under 5 feet 4 inches tall), Douglas replaced the exhausted Clay as leader of the Compromise cause in the Senate. Instead of attempting to resubmit the Compromise as a single omnibus bill, Douglas stripped it down to its five component parts and submitted each part as a separate bill. This ingenious strategy worked beautifully. Southerners voted for those proposals they liked: Northerners did likewise. A few middle-of-the-roaders, like Douglas himself, swung the balance. By September 1850, all the bits of the Compromise - many by very small majorities - had passed: statehood for California; territorial status for Utah and New Mexico, allowing popular sovereignty; resolution of the Texas-New Mexico boundary disagreement; abolition of the slave trade in the District of Columbia; and a new Fugitive Slave Act. Douglas was jubilant: 'The North has not surrendered to the South, nor has the South made any humiliating concessions to the North. Each section has maintained its honour and its rights and both have met on the common ground of justice and compromise'. Other political leaders also hailed the Compromise of 1850 as a settlement of the issues that threatened to divide the nation.

However, historians have questioned whether the 1850 Compromise was indeed a success. David Potter questioned whether it was even a compromise! He thought it was really an 'armistice'. The vast majority of Northern Congressmen had, after all, voted against the pro-slavery measures while the vast majority of Southern Congressmen had voted against the anti-slavery measures. The Compromise had skirted rather than settled, the controversy over the status of slavery in the territories, providing no formula to guide the future. Northerners continued to believe that slavery could and should be prohibited from the territories: Southerners insisted that they had the right to carry slaves into any territory before it became a state.

Many Northerners resented the new Fugitive Slave Act and believed that Congress had cravenly surrendered to Southern bluster and bluff. The fact that many Southerners claimed they had won a victory was not reassuring to Northerners. However, historians tend to the view that the North gained more than the South from the Compromise/armistice. The entry of - free - California into the Union tilted the balance in favour of the free states. The resolutions on New Mexico and Utah were hollow victories for the South. The odds were that these areas would also enter the Union as free states at some time in the future. The Fugitive Slave Act was the North's only major concession.

Congress, thanks to the efforts of men like Clay, Webster and Douglas, had averted a crisis. Most Americans seem prepared to accept the Compromise. Across the USA, there were mass meetings to celebrate its passage and to pledge support for it. The Compromise put an end to the hopes of Southern secessionists. Only half the Nashville convention delegates turned up when it met again in November. Most recognised the futility of the proceedings. It was clear that the great majority of Southerners still supported the Union. In Southern state elections in 1851-2 unionist candidates defeated secessionists even in South Carolina and Mississippi. The South had decided against secession for now - but not necessarily for ever. Ominously for the future, most Southerners had come to accept Calhoun's doctrine that secession was a valid constitutional remedy, applicable in appropriate circumstances.

The hope was that those circumstances would not arise. In December 1851 President Fillmore announced that the Compromise was 'final and irrevocable'. Many Congressmen hoped for a respite from sectional agitation. Indeed, the two years that remained of Fillmore's administration was a period of relative tranquility. It was also a period of prosperity as Americans continued to enjoy the fruits of the prolonged economic boom. But some sectional problems did remain - not least those associated with the Fugitive Slave Act.

11 The Fugitive Slave Act

The Fugitive Slave Act appalled Northern abolitionists. While some Northerners accepted it as the price the North had to pay to save the Union, the Act contained a number of features which were distasteful to moderates and outrageous to abolitionists. (For example, it denied alleged fugitives the right of trial by jury and did not allow them to testify in their own behalf.) It also authorised Federal marshals to raise posses to pursue fugitives on Northern soil. Those who refused to join risked a $1,000 fine. In addition, the law targeted not only recent runaways but also those who had fled the South decades earlier. (In 1851 slave catchers wrenched a former slave from his family in Indiana and returned him to a master from whom he had fled in 1831.) Fugitives were now only safe if they made it to Canada. Abolitionists had a field day. 'Let the President ... drench our land of freedom in blood', proclaimed Ohio's Whig Congressman Joshua Giddings, 'but he will never make us obey the law'. Frederick Douglass urged strong defiance of the Act: 'The only way to make the Fugitive Slave Law a dead letter is to make a half dozen or more dead kidnappers', he said in 1853.

Efforts to catch and return fugitive slaves inflamed feelings in both the North and South. In 1854 a Boston mob broke into a courthouse and killed a guard in an abortive effort to rescue the fugitive slave Anthony Burns. In the end Federal troops had to be sent to escort Burns to Boston harbour where a ship carried him back to slavery. (Bostonians later successfully purchased Burns's freedom!). The Burns affair was one of a number of well-publicised incidents. In response to the Act, vigilance committees sprang up in many Northern communities to help endangered blacks escape to Canada. During the 1850s nine Northern states passed new personal liberty laws. By such techniques as forbidding the use of state jails to imprison alleged fugitives, these laws were intended to make it difficult, if not impossible, to enforce Federal law.

Southerners kept a watchful eye on proceedings, regarding the Fugitive Slave Act as a test of Northern goodwill. The fact that some free states went to enormous lengths to negate it caused great resentment. However, it is likely that overt resistance to the Act was exaggerated at the time both by Southerners and abolitionists. In most Northern states the law was enforced without much trouble. Of some 200 blacks arrested in the first six years of the law, only 15 were rescued and only three of these by force. It is true that only 332 fugitive slaves were ever returned to the South from the free states in the 1850s. But this was not because of Northern resistance: it simply reflected the fact that relatively few slaves escaped North. Moreover, many Southern slave owners were not prepared to pay the huge sums involved in bringing back renegade slaves who might well disaffect other slaves. The cost of reclaiming a slave was often greater than the slave's value.

12 The Impact of *Uncle Tom's Cabin*

In 1852 Harriet Beecher Stowe published *Uncle Tom's Cabin*. The novel, which presented a fierce attack on slavery, was an immediate best-seller, selling 300,000 copies in 1852 in the USA alone and a further 2,000,000 copies in America over the next ten years. (It also sold well overseas, especially in Britain.) Even those Northerners who did not read it were familiar with its theme because it was also turned into songs and plays. Stowe herself had little first hand knowledge of the peculiar institution: she relied upon her imagination and drew heavily on abolitionist literature when describing its brutalities. Although it is impossible to gauge its precise impact, *Uncle Tom's Cabin* undoubtedly aroused wide Northern sympathy for slaves. (Stowe particularly played effectively on the emotions of her readers by demonstrating to an age that revered family life how slavery tore the family apart.) Though the novel hardly lived up to the prediction of a pro-slavery lawyer that it would convert 2,000,000 people to abolitionism, it probably did push some Northerners toward a more aggressively anti-slavery stance. In Potter's view, Northerners' attitude to slavery was 'never quite the same after *Uncle Tom's Cabin.* When President Lincoln met Stowe in 1863 he is reported to have said to her: 'So you're the little woman who wrote the book that made this great war!'

13 The 1852 Presidential Election

The Democrats, who had done well in the 1850 mid-term elections, were confident of victory in 1852. Many Irish and German immigrants were now entitled to vote and were expected to vote Democrat. Moreover, Van Buren and his New York supporters - who had formed the core of the Free Soil party in 1848 - had now returned to the Democrat fold. The Democrats main problem was finding a suitable presidential candidate. After 49 roll calls, the Democrat convention chose the 'dark horse' candidate Franklin Pierce of New Hampshire. Handsome, charming but somewhat lightweight, Pierce had served without much distinction in the Mexican War. His main advantage was that he was acceptable to all factions of the party. Although he was a Northerner, he was known to be sympathetic to Southern views. 'We 'Polked' 'em in '44', boasted the Democrat press:' we'll Pierce 'em in '52'. The Democrats campaigned on a platform supporting the 1850 Compromise, resisting 'agitation of the slavery question under whatever shape or colour the attempt may be made', and rallied behind the idea of applying popular sovereignty to all the territories.

The Whig party convention met at Baltimore. It was soon clear that the party was divided North against South, both in terms of agreeing to a platform and in terms of choosing a candidate. There were four possible candidates - President Millard Fillmore, Daniel Webster, William Seward, and General Winfield Scott, the Mexican War hero. Most Northern Whigs supported Scott, who (somewhat ironically) was a Southerner. Most Southern Whigs preferred to retain Fillmore - a Northerner. Scott was finally nominated on the 53rd ballot. In many ways he was an excellent choice. Although his forty years service in the army had given him little time to devote to politics, he was a man of great integrity and ability and the Whigs had twice won elections by nominating military heroes with little previous political interest or experience. They hoped - and expected - that this would be the third time lucky. The Whigs managed to agree on a leader: but the convention could not agree on a platform. In consequence the Whig platform, beyond feebly endorsing the 1850 Compromise, said virtually nothing. Neither Northern nor Southern Whigs were happy with the outcome. Northerners were unhappy with the platform. Southerners were unhappy with the candidate, particularly as Scott seemed to have fallen under the influence of Seward. In the campaign the Whigs made some effort to appeal to Irish and German immigrants but this policy backfired. It failed to win many Catholic voters and was strongly resented by many Protestant Americans who hated the Catholic immigrants. The result of the election was a victory for Pierce who won 1,601,274 votes (51 per cent) and carried 27 states (254 electoral college votes). Scott won 1,386,580 votes (44 per cent) but carried only 4 states (42 electoral college votes). John Hale, the Free Soil party candidate, won 156,000 votes (5 per cent), carrying not a single state.

Many Whigs were stunned by the defeat. The outcome was particularly galling for Southern Whigs. In the six states of the Lower South, Scott won only 35 per cent of the popular vote: these same states had given Taylor 50 per cent in 1848. The Whig Senator from Georgia, Alexander Stephens, moaned that 'the Whig Party is dead'. Some Northern Whigs also gave up hope that the party could ever again challenge the Democrats. This view - although soon to be proved correct - was perhaps a little premature. Scott had actually run a creditable race. While losing support in the lower South, he had retained considerable support in the upper South. Many state Whig organisations continued to hold together. Some leading Whigs, like Seward, were confident that they could heal the sectional wounds and that common hostility to the Democrats would reunite and revitalise the party.

14 President Pierce and Expansion

Franklin Pierce was inaugurated President in March 1853. Although he lacked much experience and was soon to prove himself weak and irresolute, he seemed to be in a strong position. The Democrat party had large majorities in both Houses of Congress. It also controlled many of the state governments. The economic boom continued and brought increasing prosperity to most Americans. It seemed that the Whig party would be unable to mount much of a challenge. It was seriously divided and its two best-known leaders - Webster and Clay - both died in 1852. Pierce hoped that the 1850 Compromise had settled the latent sectional conflict. He intended to maintain the unity of his party by championing expansionist policies. Although a Northerner, he sympathised with - and was influenced by - the Southern wing of his party. Given the political situation, Southerners had good reason for hoping that the United States would expand into Central America and/or Cuba, thus allowing the opportunity for slavery also to expand.

In 1853 Pierce gave emissary James Gadsden the authority to negotiate for the purchase of 250,000 square miles of territory from Mexico. Gadsden's mission had limited success, finally concluding a treaty with Mexico for the purchase of a strip of land of some 54,000 square miles. Southerners favoured the acquisition of this territory, not because of its slavery potential, but because it would assist the building of a Southern railway to the Pacific. The negative Northern reaction to the Gadsden Purchase indicated the mounting suspicion of Southern expansionist aims - as well as opposition to a Southern trans-continental railway route. Gadsden's treaty only gained Senate approval in 1854 after an amendment slashed 9,000 square miles from the proposed purchase.

Pierce encountered even more serious sectional buffeting when he tried to acquire the island of Cuba, the last remnant of Spain's American empire. In 1851 an American-sponsored 'filibuster' (unofficial military) expedition to try to overthrow the Spanish Cuban government had failed miserably. The Spanish authorities treated the Cuban rebels and their American allies severely: 50 American mercenaries were shot by firing squad. In 1853-4 Mississippi's former Senator John Quitman planned an even greater filibustering expedition to seize Cuba. Several thousand American volunteers were recruited and contact made with Cuban rebels to co-ordinate another rebellion. Prominent Southerners endorsed Quitman's project. In July 1853 President Pierce met Quitman and - unofficially - encouraged him to go ahead with his plans. Pierce himself wanted to purchase Cuba - but may have encouraged Quitman, hoping to spark a Texas-style revolt in the island or as a way to scare Spain into selling. The main problem as far as Pierce was concerned was Northern opinion: many Northerners viewed filibustering as another manifestation of a Slave Power conspiracy to grab more territory for slavery. Pierce, alarmed by Northern Democrat reaction and by signs that Spain planned to defend Cuba, changed his tune and forced Quitman to scuttle his planned expedition.

Still hoping to purchase Cuba, Pierce authorised Soule, the American minister in Spain, to offer as much as $130 million for the island. If the offer was turned down, Soule was then to direct his effort 'to the next desirable object which is to detach that island from the Spanish dominion'. Events, however, quickly slipped out of Pierce's control. In October 1854 the American ministers to Britain and France met in Belgium and issued the unofficial Ostend Manifesto. This stated that Cuba 'is as necessary to the North American Republic as any of its present members' and called upon the United States to make an 'immediate and earnest effort' to buy the island: if Spain refused to sell, then the USA would be 'justified in wresting it from Spain'. Unfortunately for Pierce, details of the Ostend Manifesto were leaked to the public and immediately denounced by Northern politicians. Faced by Northern outrage at the threat of war against Spain, Pierce quickly repudiated the Manifesto and Soule resigned.

The hopes of Pierce and Southern expansionists thus came to nothing. The expansionist efforts simply created enough commotion to worry Northerners that the South aspired to establish a Latin American slave empire. Many (but by no means all) Southerners did so aspire -

and remained optimistic about their aspirations - throughout the 1850s.

15 Conclusion

Events before and after 1846 had shown that expansion created grave dangers for the American Union. Expansion could all too easily ignite sectional jealousies and result in confrontations. In 1849-50 a large number of Southerners had actually talked in terms of seceding from the Union. The 1850 Compromise had managed to contain the immediate danger - but had not resolved the problem of slavery expansion. The fact that both the Whigs and Democrats were national parties, each with widespread popular support in North and South, had generally helped maintain sectional harmony. Leading politicians had often done their best to play down sectional animosity in order to avoid dividing their parties. In 1852 the Presidential candidates Franklin Pierce and Winfield Scott had each won support in both North and South. But Pierce was to be the last presidential candidate for 80 years to win the popular and electoral vote in both sections. The political situation after 1852 was to result in the collapse of the second party system and the disintegration of the Whig party. The reasons for - and the consequences of - that collapse are issues which will be examined in detail in the next chapter.

Making notes on 'The Impact of the Mexican War'

This chapter is designed to show the political problems posed to the United States by Western expansion. Somewhat ironically, these problems largely arose because of the United States' success in the Mexican War. The headings used in this chapter should help you to organise the material and compile a detailed summary of the main events from 1846 to 1853. Try to expand the final section ('Conclusion') by attempting to formulate your own judgements about the period. As a means of doing this, you might briefly answer the following questions:
1   To what extent was the Mexican War to blame for the United States sectional problems?
2   Was popular sovereignty a sensible notion?
3   How successful was the 1850 Compromise?
4   Did secession and/or Civil War seem at all imminent in 1852-3?

Source-based questions on 'The Impact of the Mexican War'

1 The 1850 Compromise: Clay and Webster
Read carefully the extracts from Clay and Webster's speeches in 1850, given on pages 59 and 60-61. Answer the following questions:
a)   What was the main concern of both Clay and Webster? (3 marks)

b) On what other issues were both Clay and Webster in agreement?
    (3 marks)
c) What were both men hoping to achieve by their speeches? (4 marks)
d) What might have been the response of a Northern abolitionist?
    (5 marks?)

2 The 1850 Compromise: Calhoun

Read carefully the extract from Calhoun's speech on pages 59-60.
Answer the following questions:
a) On what issues might Clay, Webster and Calhoun have agreed?
    (4 marks)
b) On what issues would Clay, Webster and Calhoun have disagreed?
    (5 marks)
c) What was Calhoun hoping to achieve by his speech? (5 marks)
d) What might have been the response of a Northern abolitionist?
    (6 marks)

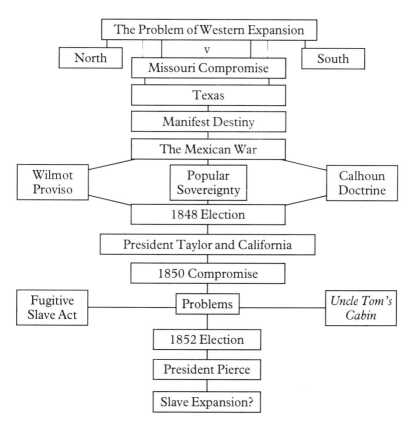

Summary - The Impact of the Mexican War

CHAPTER 5

The Rise of the Republican Party

1 Introduction

From the 1830s to the early 1850s American politics had been dominated by the Democrats and the Whigs. These parties drew upon national - not sectional - support. While the Democrat party was usually strongest in the South, large numbers of Southerners voted Whig. Northerners tended to be equally divided between Democrats and Whigs. As long as men placed loyalty to their party ahead of sectional loyalty neither North nor South could easily be united one against the other. But in the mid-1850s the second party system collapsed. While the Democrat party survived, the Whig party disintegrated. The Republican party - a purely sectional party which drew support only from Northerners - finally emerged to challenge the Democrats. The election of the first Republican President, Abraham Lincoln, in November 1860 was to spark secession and Civil War.

Understanding why the second party system collapsed is thus of major importance in understanding why the Civil War occurred. The problem of slavery expansion is usually seen as the crucial issue and the 1854 Kansas-Nebraska Act the vital catalyst. However, while not necessarily denying the importance of slavery expansion or the Kansas-Nebraska Act, historians have recently focused on other important factors, not least the concern felt by many Americans at the flood of Catholic immigrants pouring into the USA in the late 1840s and early 1850s. Northern voters seem to have lost faith in the established parties' ability to tackle the main issues of the day. New parties appeared, first destroying the Whig party and then stepping into the vacuum left by its demise. One of these parties - the Republican party - was mainly concerned with the slavery expansion issue. Another - the Know Nothing (or American) party - was mainly concerned with nativist and anti-immigrant issues. Until the 1856 presidential election it was far from clear which party - and which issues - would dominate the Northern political scene. This chapter will examine why the Republican party emerged as the main challenger to the Democrat party.

2 The Problem of Kansas-Nebraska

Nebraska was the remaining part of the Louisiana Purchase. A vast, arid territory, it was still unsettled by white Americans in the early 1850s. Settlers were anxious to move in but could not legally buy land until Congress first organised the area into a territory, enabling the land to be surveyed and put up for sale. In addition, railway promoters were anxious to build a line through Nebraska to the Pacific coast. This also necessitated the area being organised into a territory. While most Northerners (particularly those in the Mid-west) were keen to see Nebraska developed, Southerners were less enthusiastic. Nebraska lay north of latitude 36°.30 and, by the terms of the Missouri Compromise, all new states in the area would eventually enter the Union as free states. Southerners, moreover, supported a Southern trans-continental railway route. Southern politicians, therefore.

This was the background to the Kansas-Nebraska bill, introduced into Congress in January 1854, by Senator Stephen Douglas, the Chairman of the Senate Committee on Territories. Douglas, Democrat Senator from Illinois and one of the main architects of the 1850 Compromise, was a man of talent, resource, energy and (presidential) ambition. He had pushed - unsuccessfully - for the organisation of Nebraska since 1844. However, Douglas knew that to get a Nebraska Bill enacted he needed the support of some Southern Senators. He also knew that those Southerners were likely to drive a hard bargain. Indeed Southerners were only likely to vote for Douglas's bill if they felt they had a chance of expanding slavery in the area: this meant that the 1820

—— Missouri Compromise line 36° 30'	ARK. Arkansas	MD. Maryland
	ALA. Alabama	MINN. Minnesota Territory
	CA. California	MISS. Mississippi
☐ Free state or territory	CONN. Connecticut	NJ. New Jersey
	FLA. Florida	NH. New Hampshire
☐ Slave state or territory	GA. Georgia	N.C. North Carolina
	IN. Indian Territory	NY. New York
☐ Territory open to slavery by principle of popular sovereignty compromise of 1850	IND. Indiana	PA. Pennsylvania
	ILL. Illinois	R.I. Rhode Island
	KY. Kentucky	S.C. South Carolina
	LA. Louisiana	TENN. Tennessee
☐ Opened to slavery by principle of popular sovereignty, Kansas - Nebraska Act 1854	MASS. Massachusetts	VT. Vermont
	MICH. Michigan	WA. Washington Territory
	MO. Missouri	WIS. Wisconsin
	ME. Maine	

The Kansas-Nebraska Bill 1854

Missouri Compromise ban would have to be by-passed in order to get the bill through Congress. Douglas's original bill, while avoiding all mention of the Missouri Compromise, was designed to appeal to the South. The entire area of Nebraska was to be organised into a single territory. The states eventually formed from it were to be received into the Union 'with or without slavery as their constitution may prescribe at the time of their admission'. The bill, which substituted popular sovereignty for the Missouri Compromise, obviously gave the South some hope of establishing slavery in Nebraska.

However, Douglas's bill did not satisfy Southern Senators. A number, including Senator David Atchison of Missouri, an outspoken defender of Southern rights, made it clear to Douglas that if he wanted Nebraska organised, his bill must specifically repeal the Missouri Compromise. An amendment to that effect was introduced and Douglas reluctantly agreed to it. He also agreed to another change. The new Kansas-Nebraska Bill divided the Nebraska territory into two: Kansas - the area immediately west of Missouri; and Nebraska - the area west of Iowa and Minnesota. There was little chance of slavery taking hold in Nebraska. But it did seem possible it might spread to Kansas.

Douglas was aware that the Kansas-Nebraska issue was delicate. A dedicated patriot, he had no wish to heighten sectional tension. Indeed, he was confident that his bill, introduced two years before the next presidential election, would cause no great strain. Although in theory slavery could now expand northwards it was highly unlikely, given geographical and climatic factors, that it would do so. Douglas, a great believer in popular sovereignty, saw no problem in letting the people of Kansas-Nebraska (or indeed any territory) decide their own fate. He was confident that they would not vote for slavery. A supporter of manifest destiny, Douglas did not want the settlement of the west to be stalled by sectional controversy. Such controversy could also prevent the building of a northern trans-continental railway which would have to run through Kansas-Nebraska. Such a railway would benefit Douglas personally: he owned considerable real estate in Chicago, which would increase in value if a trans-continental railway, terminating in Chicago, was built.

Douglas had other motives. He believed there was political capital to be gained from his Kansas-Nebraska measure. It should enhance his reputation in his home state of Illinois, where many people stood to benefit from a trans-continental railway leading west from Chicago (rather than from St Louis or New Orleans). Settlement of the Nebraska issue would also enhance his presidential ambitions. Already the acknowledged champion of North-western interests, the Kansas-Nebraska Bill should increase his standing among Southern Democrats. He hoped that the Democrat party could rally behind the idea of popular sovereignty and that this - and western expansion - would be vote-winning issues in 1856.

Douglas believed he had succeeded in winning over the South

without conceding much in return. However, he seriously miscalculated. His bill, far from healing North-South tension, created a 'hell of a
storm' throughout the North. It was proof to many Northerners that the
Slave Power conspiracy was still at work. Douglas, himself, was depicted
as a Northern 'doughface' - a traitor to his section.

One of the most effective pieces of abolitionist propaganda was a
tract, written by Salmon Chase, entitled 'The Appeal of the
Independent Democrats in Congress to the People of the United
States', published in January 1854. Here is an extract.

1 We arraign this bill as a gross violation of a sacred pledge; as a
  criminal betrayal of precious rights; as part and parcel of an
  atrocious plot to exclude from the vast unoccupied region
  immigrants from the Old World and free labourers from our own
5 states and convert it into a dreary region of despotism, inhabited by
  masters and slaves. Take your maps, fellow citizens, we entreat
  you, and see what country it is which this bill gratuitously and
  recklessly proposes to open to slavery ... This immense region,
  occupying the very heart of the North American Continent, and
10 larger, by thirty-three thousand square miles, than all the existing
  free States ... this immense region the bill now before the Senate,
  without reason and without excuse, but in flagrant disregard of
  sound policy and sacred faith, purposes to open to slavery ...
      We appeal to the people. We warn you that the dearest interests
15 of freedom and the Union are in imminent peril. Demagogues may
  tell you that the Union can be maintained only by submitting to the
  demands of slavery. We tell you that the Union can only be
  maintained by the full recognition of the just claims of freedom and
  man.

The following extract from a sermon by the abolitionist preacher
Theodore Parker, delivered in February 1854, is another example of the
North's response to Douglas's measure:

1 The Slave Power has long been seeking to extend its jurisdiction. It
  has eminently succeeded. It fills all the chief offices of the nation;
  the Presidents are Slave Presidents; the Supreme Court is of Slave
  Judges, every one ... In all that depends on the political action of
5 America, the Slave Power carries the day. In what depends on
  industry, population, education, it is the North. The Slave Power
  seeks to extend its institutions at the expense of humanity. The
  North works with it ... So the question is, shall we let Slavery into
  the two great territories of Kansas and Nebraska? That is a
10 question of economy. Here it is. Shall men work with poor
  industrial tools, or with good ones? Shall they have the varied

industry of New England and the North, or the Slave labour of Virginia and Carolina? Shall their land be worth five dollars and a half as in South Carolina, or thirty dollars and a half as in
15 Connecticut? Shall the people all be comfortable, engaged in honest work, which enriches while it elevates; or shall a part be the poorest of the world that a few may be idle and rich?

Initially most Southerners had been apathetic about the Kansas-Nebraska Bill. But the ferocity of Northern attacks led to a Southern counter-attack. Passage of the bill suddenly became a symbol of Southern honour. The result was a great struggle in Congress. Northern Free Soilers, Democrats and Whigs joined forces in opposition to it, and previously marginalised abolitionists suddenly exerted considerable influence. Southern Whigs and Democrats united in supporting the bill. President Pierce's administration, unable to risk losing the South, agreed to make it a test of party loyalty, thus ensuring that some Northern Democrats would support the measure. After months of bitter debate, the bill passed through both houses of Congress (the Senate voted 37 to 14 in its favour: the House 115 to 104) and became law in May 1854. What was now the Kansas-Nebraska Act had effectively sectionalised Congress. 90 per cent of all Southerners in Congress had voted for it: 64 per cent of all Northerners had voted against it. The Northern Democrats had splintered: 44 in the House voted for it: 43 voted against it.

In the summer of 1854 Douglas, delighted that both Kansas and Nebraska could now set up territorial governments, was still confident that the sectional storm would be short-lived and that the Democrats would retain their strength in the North, particularly as the Whig party seemed in total disarray. However, in reality, Douglas had little cause for optimism. By failing to predict the extent of the Northern outrage generated by his Act, he weakened his party, damaged his own presidential ambitions and revived North-South rivalry. Many Northern Democrats were to drift away from the party after 1854, ensuring that the party was increasingly dominated by its Southern wing. The collapse of the Whig party, far from helping the Democrats, was to result (eventually) in the rise of the Republican party. Even Douglas's hope of establishing a railway through the Kansas-Nebraska territory was not to be realised in his lifetime.

3 The Collapse of the Second Party System

The 1854 mid-term elections were a disaster for the Democrats. Before 1854 the party had been strong in both North and South. Indeed, in the 1852-4 Congress 91 Democrats represented free states and 67 Democrats represented slave states. But in the 1854 elections the free state Democrats suffered crushing reverses, losing all but 23 of their seats. (In the South it was a different story. Here the Democrats retained all but 4 of the 67 seats previously held.) Democrats also lost control of most Northern state legislatures: in 1852 the Democrats had won all but two of the Northern states; in 1854 they lost all but two.

Prior to 1854 the Whig party would have benefited from the unpopularity of the Democrats in the North. Some leading Northern Whigs, like Seward, expected to do so. In 1854 Whigs in several Northern states confidently campaigned on an anti-Nebraska platform, hoping that Northern voters would repudiate the Democrats who were blamed for sponsoring the Kansas-Nebraska Act. But there was little reason for Whig optimism. By the mid-term elections the Whig party was no longer a serious force in many Northern states. New parties had arisen attracting mass support. The rise of these parties led to both the speedy demise of the Whig party and the weakening of Democrat loyalties throughout the North.

Until recently the collapse of the Whig party was usually seen as the direct result of the sectional crisis resulting from the Kansas-Nebraska Act. This undoubtedly set Southern Whigs against Northern Whigs (in the same way that it set Southern against Northern Democrats). However, while divisions over slavery certainly played a part in the collapse of the Whig party, other factors were also crucially important. There seems little doubt that the Whig decline began in several Northern states well before the debates over Kansas-Nebraska. In the early 1850s the Whigs had done badly, both nationally (in 1852) and at state level. State and local elections in 1853 were a disaster for the Northern Whigs. Historians Michael Holt and William Gienapp have argued (convincingly) that the main problem confronting both Northern Whigs and Democrats at local level in the early 1850s was not the slavery question but the rise of 'ethnocultural' issues. These issues were essentially temperance, anti-immigration and anti-Catholicism. All three issues were linked.

Temperance had become a major political matter in the 1840s. Alcohol was seen as a dangerous drug: prohibition, it was hoped, would solve many of the country's most serious social problems, especially crime and welfare-dependence. In 1851 Maine became the first state to ban the manufacture and sale of alcoholic beverages. A further 12 Northern states soon enacted similar prohibition measures. While Democrats generally opposed 'Maine laws', the Whig party was divided. The groups that most opposed temperance tended to be recent Catholic immigrants from Ireland and Germany. Both peoples had a reputation for heavy drinking and were quite happy to do so on Sundays. Supporters of temperance tended to be native Americans, most of whom disliked Catholicism and the growing influx of immigrants.

Between 1845 and 1854 some 3,000,000 immigrants entered the USA. Over 1,000,000 of these were Irish Catholics, most of whom were escaping the horrors of the Irish potato famine. German Catholics ran the Irish a close second. (By the early 1850s there were more German immigrants than Irish.) The failure of the 1848 revolutions in Germany does not seem to have been a major factor in sparking the German flood (as historians once thought). Few German immigrants were escaping persecution: most simply wanted to better themselves. Many had sufficient funds to trek west to states like Wisconsin and Minnesota where they were able to purchase farms. The Irish, with fewer resources, tended to settle in the cities of the North-east.

Both the German and (particularly) the Irish Catholics seemed to threaten the traditional values of the United States. Fear of a papal plot to subvert and control the USA was deep-rooted among native-born Americans, the majority of whom were strongly Protestant. Many Protestants were horrified by the growth of Catholicism. (Between 1850 and 1854 the number of Catholic bishops, priests and Churches almost doubled.) The growing political power of Catholic voters, particularly in cities like New York and Boston, was also resented by native-born Americans. In Boston, the immigrant vote increased by 195 per cent in the five years after 1850: the native-born vote rose by only 14 per cent. Most Catholics voted Democrat. They did so because the Democrat party seemed more in tune with their interests: it was opposed to both temperance laws and restrictions on immigrants' rights. Many native-born Americans feared that the Irish voted en masse as their political bosses - or their priests - told them. This was seen as a threat to democracy and the very basis of what it meant to be American.

Native Americans did not just have religious and political concerns: there were also unpleasant social and economic consequences of mass immigration. Irishmen and women provided a source of cheap labour, pulling down wage levels and taking jobs from native-born workers. Native Americans also associated Irish immigrants with increased crime and welfare costs. In Cincinnati the crime rate tripled between 1846 and 1853 and the murder rate increased seven fold. In Boston poor relief expenditure rose three fold in the same period. Such figures were typical. Native-born Americans often blamed the immigrants for everything they thought wrong in society.

Given that the vast majority of Irish and German Catholics voted Democrat, there was no way that the Democrat party was ever likely to support temperance, anti-immigrant or anti-Catholic measures. Indeed the Democrat party went out of its way to woo the immigrant vote, nominating and appointing Catholic officeholders. The Whig party was the only party likely to take a stance on ethno-cultural issues. However, in the early 1850s the Whigs, both at local and national level, failed to respond to the wishes of nativist voters. Some Whig leaders were fearful of alienating 'wet' voters. Others, like Seward, thought the party ought to go out of its way to try to capture the growing immigrant vote. In the 1852 presidential election some Whigs had been actively pro-Catholic (and anti-prohibition). The reasoning behind this Whig strategy was understandable - given the importance of the immigrant vote. But the strategy failed to win the election: few Irish were persuaded to vote Whig; and some traditional Whig voters stayed at home rather than vote for a party which seemed to be trying to appease Catholics. Moreover, the strategy alienated nativist voters (many of whom still voted Whig in 1852 because there was no alternative) just at the time when anti-Catholic sentiment was rising.

Holt has claimed that the anti-immigrant views of many Northerners was attributable to fear and grievance generated by disruptive economic and social forces at work in the early 1850s. He has particularly cited the disturbing effects of the massive railway construction from 1849 to 1854 which brought immigrant construction crews into areas which had previously not seen a foreigner. Railways, moreover, destroyed or threatened the traditional jobs of some workers and also brought isolated communities into contact with the outside world. This economic explanation, while interesting, is not altogether convincing. The early 1850s were boom years for most Americans. Recession, which might have been expected to have generated anti-immigrant feeling, did not set in until 1857 and did not result in increased nativist tension.

Holt has also claimed - and this claim is far more justified - that many Northern voters in the early 1850s had become alienated from both the old political parties. Both Whig and Democrat politicians failed to speak with conviction on what many perceived to be the major issues of the day: immigration, temperance and slavery expansion. Increasingly, in Holt's view, the 'old guard' politicians seemed more concerned with the spoils of office than with principle - and this at a time when many Northerners saw their cherished republicanism under threat whether from the Southern Slave Power or Catholics or both. Angry and frustrated with both their Whig and Democrat representatives, the Northern electorate began to look to new parties which would more militantly represent their views. This happened first at state and local level. Disintegration of loyalty to the old parties in 1853 had little to do with sectional conflict between North and South: indeed it occurred during a temporary lull in that conflict.

4 The Know Nothings

Concern about temperance, immigration and expanding Catholicism resulted in the rise of a nativist movement whose members were usually referred to as Know Nothings. The Know Nothing order was an offshoot of the Order of the Star-Spangled Banner, a secret nativist society formed in New York in 1849. In the early 1850s the Know Nothing movement, similar in some ways to the Masonic movement, suddenly mushroomed. One of the key figures in its rise was James Barker who helped set up hundreds of Know Nothing lodges, first in New York and then all over the United States. As membership grew, an elaborate structure was created with local lodges, state councils, and a grand national council. Know Nothing members, who pledged to vote for no-one except native-born Protestants, learned rituals, grips and passwords as they were initiated to different degrees of membership. When asked questions about the order, they were supposed to reply, 'I know nothing', thereby giving the movement its name.

The Know Nothing order first entered politics by secretly backing its own members or throwing its support behind suitable candidates from the tickets of the existing parties. It had so much success that by 1854 the movement came out into the open and took on the characteristics of a political party, usually selecting its own candidates. Local Know Nothing lodges seem to have had considerable influence over which candidate they would support or select. In 1853-4 rank and file members often chose men who had little previous political experience and who were not, therefore, tarnished by association with the Whig and Democrat political machines. The Know Nothings were thus able to represent themselves as being a genuine people's party. (In some Midwestern states the parties that Know Nothings joined and dominated were referred to as the 'People's Party'). The Know Nothing political agenda varied from time to time and place to place. However, most Know Nothings wanted checks on immigration, legislation preventing (what was seen as) the dumping of European paupers and criminals in the USA, strict laws restricting office-holding to native-born citizens, and a 21 years probationary period before immigrants could become naturalized American citizens and thus vote.

Several events aided the Know Nothing cause in 1853. One was Catholic attempts to influence the teaching in public schools and set up their own schools. Protestants saw these moves as the thin end of the wedge. Once Catholics had their own schools, they would be a cancer within the body politic - a state within a state. A second was President Pierce's appointment of James Campbell, a Catholic, as Postmaster General (a post with massive patronage powers). The visit of the Papal nuncio Archbishop Bedini to the USA in June 1853 seemed further evidence of a Catholic plot. Wherever he went Bedini was pursued by protestors and his appearance caused riots in several cities.

Although attracted by its anti-Catholic and anti-immigrant stance, Northerners joined the Know Nothing movement for a variety of other reasons. Some approved of its anti-establishment stand and its promise to return power to the people. Some liked its temperance stand. Others joined because they hated the Democrat party and in many states the Know Nothings became the Democrats' main opponents. The unpopularity of the Kansas-Nebraska Act, associated with the Democrat party, also helped the Know Nothings. Inevitably the Know Nothings won the support of many ex-Whigs. Indeed leading Democrats initially thought the Know Nothings were essentially an arm of the Whig party. But they soon discovered that members of their own party were streaming into Know Nothing lodges as well. The Know Nothings seem to have also attracted first-time and previously uncommitted voters.

A letter from a Detroit judge to Supreme Court Justice John McLean in 1855 indicates why so many Americans joined the Know Nothings.

1 You know that for the last quarter of a century political traders and gamesters have so manufactured public opinion, and so directed party organisation, that our Union has been endangered and bad men elevated to place and power, contrary to the true sentiment of
5 the People. And there seemed to be no hope for us. Both parties courted what was called the foreign vote; and the highest aspirants of the Senate, to ensure success, strove which could pay more homage to a foreign prince, whose ecclesiastical subjects, constituted so large a portion of this *imperium in imperio*. The Papal
10 Power at Rome, apprised fully of this state of things, gave direction to her vassal priesthood, to use their supposed power for the propaganda files, and hence the attack on our school systems in Cincinnati, New York, Baltimore, and Detroit. I give thanks to God, that they commenced the warfare at the time they did, and
15 that their plan was discerned and defeated.

By 1854 the Know Nothings probably had over 1,000,000 members and began to wield real political power. In June 1854 the entire Know Nothing ticket was elected in the Philadelphia municipal elections. The movement went on to win 63 per cent of the vote in Massachusetts, electing all the state officers and all its congressmen. In 1855 the Know Nothings won control of three more New England states and also made significant advances in Pennsylvania and New York. The movement even began to win large-scale support, mainly from ex-Whigs, in the South. By 1855 the Know Nothing order, now calling itself the American party, held open conventions on a state and national level.

Once in office the Know Nothings concerned themselves with nativist matters. In Massachusetts, for example, the legislature banned the teaching of foreign languages. It set up a nunnery committee because it believed that nunneries were used by Catholic priests for sexual misconduct. Literacy tests (for voting) were introduced, hoping to reduce the immigrant vote. In 1855 the Massachusetts legislature approved an amendment to the state constitution barring anyone owing allegiance to any 'foreign prince, power or potentate' from holding government office. But the Know Nothings were not simply a one-issue party. In an effort to represent the wishes of working-class voters, the Massachusetts legislature also supported 'progressive' economic and social measures including the advancement of women's rights, prison reform and a maximum ten hour day for working men. Temperance legislation was also part of the Know Nothing package.

5 The Republican Party

However, in 1854 the Northern electorate was not just concerned with ethno-cultural issues. The Kansas-Nebraska Act awakened the spectre of the Slave Power and many Northerners were keen to give support to parties opposed to the expansion of slavery. Efforts to establish 'fusion' parties of Free Soilers, Whigs and Democrats committed to opposing the Slave Power proved to be more difficult than many politicians had expected, partly because so many Northerners seemed more concerned with nativist issues. Nevertheless, in the spring and summer of 1854 a number of anti-slavery coalitions were formed, especially in the Midwestern states. These coalitions went under a variety of names. In Indiana and Ohio they called themselves the People's Party. Elsewhere they were known as the Anti-Nebraska Party. In Michigan and Wisconsin, the anti-slavery coalitions called themselves Republicans. As the months passed it was the Republican name which caught on.

By the end of 1854 it was not clear whether the Know Nothings or Republicans would pick up the tattered Whig mantle in the North. In general, the Republicans were strongest in the Midwest: the Know Nothings were strongest in New England and the east. However, in most Northern states the two parties were not necessarily in competition: indeed they often tried to avoid a contest. Many - perhaps most - Northerners were both anti-immigrant and anti-slavery: they hated the Church of Rome, the Slave Power and the Democrat party which seemed to support both immigrants and slavery.

However, by no means all Republicans were ready to work with the Know Nothings. Some denounced nativism, seeing it as bigotry and as a red-herring. Abraham Lincoln, an ex-Whig who was moving into the Republican camp, described his views as follows in August 1855:

1 I am not a Know-Nothing. That is certain. How can I be? How can any one who abhors the oppression of negroes, be in favour of degrading classes of white people? Our progress in degeneracy appears to me to be pretty rapid. As a nation, we began by
5 declaring that 'all men are created equal'. We now practically read it 'all men are created equal except negroes'. When the Know-Nothings get control, it will read 'all men are created equal, except negroes, and foreigners, and catholics'. When it comes to this, I should prefer emigrating to some country where they make
10 no pretence of loving liberty - to Russia, for instance, where despotism can be taken pure, and without the base alloy of hypocrisy.

Given the Democrat reverses in the North in the 1854 elections, it was clear that there would be anti-Democrat majority in the Congress which met in December 1855. But precisely which groups the 150 or so anti-Democrat Congressmen supported remained to be seen. Many anti-Nebraska (i.e. Republican) politicians were Know Nothings and vice-versa. For those 'pure' anti-Nebraska politicians who were opposed to nativism, the 1854 elections had been a disappointing set-back. Know Nothing strength seemed a major roadblock to the establishment of a powerful Republican party. In 1854-5 it was still far from certain which issue - anti-slavery or anti-immigration - would dominate the political agenda. The rise of the Republican party was thus far from inevitable - or obvious. Indeed, most political observers expected the Know Nothings to be the main opponents of the Democrats in the 1856 presidential election. Given its concerns, the Republican party could never be more than a Northern sectional party. In contrast, the Know Nothing order, with a strong Northern power-base and growing support in the South, was a national movement. But as it turned out, Southern expansion was to prove an Achilles heel for the Know Nothings. Events in Kansas also came to the rescue of the Republicans.

6 The Situation in Kansas, 1854-6

After the Kansas-Nebraska Act, people began to move into Kansas. The main concern of most settlers, as everywhere in the West, was land and water rights. However, for Northern and Southern politicians far more was at stake. Northerners thought that if slavery expanded into Kansas it might expand anywhere. Southerners, in contrast, believed that developments in Kansas might be crucial to the very existence of slavery. These feelings were well expressed in impassioned debates in the Senate in 1854. Seward from New York threw down the gauntlet to the South: 'We will engage in competition for the virgin soil of Kansas and God give the victory to the side which is stronger in numbers as it is in right'. Senator Atchison of Missouri was only too ready to take up the challenge. 'We are playing for a mighty stake; if we win we carry slavery to the Pacific Ocean; if we fail, we lose Missouri, Arkansas and Texas and all the territories; the game must be played boldly'. George Badger of North Carolina expressed the following opinion: 'If some southern gentleman wishes to take the ... old woman that nursed him in childhood and whom he called 'Mammy'... into one of these new Territories for the betterment of the fortunes of his whole family, why in the name of God, should anybody prevent it?' Benjamin Wade from Ohio, an ardent abolitionist, responded: 'We have not the least objection to the Senator's migrating to Kansas and taking his old mammy along with him. We only insist that he shall not be empowered to sell her after taking her there'.

While most Northerners and Southerners watched developments in Kansas, a number also tried to influence them. Eli Thayer, for example, set up a Massachusetts Emigrant Aid Company in 1854, intending to encourage Northerners to settle in Kansas. The Company, which offered advice and money, had some, albeit limited, success: 650 settlers were sponsored by the Company in 1854 and a further 1000 in 1855. However, in the short term, pro-slavers seemed to be in the strongest position if only because many of the first Kansas settlers came from the slave state of Missouri. Here Senator Atchison formed the Platte County Defensive Association which was pledged to ensure that Kansas became a slave state. He recommended that his fellow Missourians defend their (slave) interests 'with the bayonet and with blood'.

Maintaining law and order in Kansas was never likely to be easy. Violence was common in all new territories. The slavery issue exacerbated matters. In October 1854 President Pierce appointed Andrew Reeder, a pro-slave Democrat, as governor of the territory. It was soon clear that the job was beyond him. In October 1854 the first 'elections' - in so far as that word can be used to describe what occurred - were held in Kansas to choose a delegation to represent the territory in Washington. 'Residents', however recently arrived, were allowed to vote. This meant that pro-slavers from Missouri could move into Kansas, vote and then return home. In consequence, the pro-slavers won a convincing victory. The 'invasion' of the 'Border Ruffians' from Missouri seemed to make a mockery of local self-government.

In March 1855 Kansas elected its first territorial legislature. The legislature would decide on the subject of slavery: the elections were thus seen as crucial. 'There are 1100 coming over from Platte County to vote and if that ain't enough we can send 5,000 - enough to kill every God-damned abolitionist in the Territory', declared Atchison. The fact that hundreds of pro-slavery Missourians did cross into Kansas to vote was probably a tactical mistake. In the spring of 1855 the pro-slavers would probably have won anyway. The fact that so many Missourians voted again tarnished the concept of popular sovereignty and cast doubt on the pro-slavery victory.

Governor Reeder, critical of proceedings, ordered new elections in a third of the districts. Free state candidates carried most of these. Nevertheless the legislature which met at Lecompton in June 1855 was dominated by pro-slavers: so much so that the free state candidates, including those who had won in the newly contested elections, were expelled. In the end only one free state representative remained and he soon resigned. The legislature proceeded to pass a series of tough pro-slavery laws. It became a capital offence to give aid to a fugitive slave. Anyone who held slavery was not legal could be imprisoned. Office-holding was restricted to avowed pro-slavery men. These measures aroused the anger of Northern public opinion. Even moderates were outraged: 'There is no doubt that some of the statutes passed by the legislature of Kansas are a disgrace to the age and the country', said Democrat Lewis Cass. Reeder, similarly appalled, vetoed some of the pro-slavery legislation. His vetoes, however, were overridden by the Kansas legislature which went on to petition for the governor's dismissal. President Pierce complied and Reeder was replaced by Wilson Shannon, a solid pro-slavery man.

Meanwhile, the free soil settlers, denying the validity of the pro-slavery legislature, set up their own government at Topeka and went on to draft their own constitution - which outlawed slavery in Kansas. By the end of 1855 most observers were certain that the majority of people in Kansas aligned with the Topeka regime. Interestingly, there were deep divisions among the free-staters, especially between 'moderates' and 'fanatics'. The (minority) 'fanatics' held abolitionist views and supported the Republican position. The 'moderates', on the other hand, were not dissimilar to the pro-slavers. Most were openly racist: one of the main reasons they opposed slavery in Kansas was that it would result in an influx of blacks. The Topeka government, dominated by moderates, actually banned blacks, slave or free, from Kansas. Friction between the two Kansas governments was inevitable because neither recognised the laws of the other as binding or its officials as legal. Northern groups, anticipating an armed struggle, sent more weapons to help the free-staters. The Southern response was just as determined. Missourians, most of whom were already well-armed, moved into Kansas to help the pro-slavers.

In May 1856 events began to turn nasty. A pro-slavery posse, trying to arrest free soil leaders, 'sacked' Lawrence (a free-state centre). This event was blown up out of all proportion by Northern journalists who invented facts to fit their stories. According to the first reports dozens of free-staters were killed in the 'attack'. In reality there were no casualties (except a member of the pro-slave 'army' who was killed when a burning building collapsed on him). Nevertheless the pro-slavers did demolish a hotel, two newspaper officers and a few houses and shops.

The Lawrence raid sparked off more serious violence. The man largely responsible for this was John Brown. Brown, a fervent abolitionist, had arrived in Kansas in October 1853. Despite a terrible business record (at least fifteen of his ventures had failed), he was sustained by his belief that God had ordained his misfortunes to test him. He was also convinced that God wanted him to punish pro-slavers. Brown had two noticeable attributes. One was an ability to father children: his twenty children provided him with his own private army. The second was an ability to inspire loyalty. By 1856 Brown was determined to strike a blow against slavery. 'Without the shedding of blood', said Brown, 'there is no remission of sins'. The shedding of blood came in May 1856 at Pottawotomie Creek. Brown, with four of his sons, a son-in-law and one other man, dragged five young pro-slavery settlers from their cabins and murdered them in cold blood. (Brown shot some of his victims: others were hacked to pieces with a broadsword.) Northern newspapers, suppressing the facts, claimed that Brown had acted in righteous self-defence. Overnight, as a result of a heinous crime, Brown became a Northern hero.

The attack on Lawrence and the massacre at Pottawotomie led to a worsening of the tension and a series of tit-for-tat killings. It was difficult for Kansanian settlers to remain neutral. Both pro-slavers and free-staters threatened, marched and counter-marched. The Northern press again exaggerated the situation, describing it as civil war. With events seemingly drifting out of control, Pierce chose a new Kansas governor - John Geary. Geary proved a good choice. Acting with authority and determination (and helped by the fact that both sides in Kansas wanted peace), he managed to patch up a truce between the warring factions.

Events in Kansas were important not simply for themselves. They served to increase tensions between North and South. The events - and the distorted reporting of them - very much boosted Republican fortunes. 'Bleeding Kansas' became a rallying cry for Northerners opposed to what they perceived to be the Slave Power at work.

7 The Decline of the Know Nothings

Despite events in Kansas, the Know Nothings remained strong throughout 1855 and into 1856. The Know Nothings supported American party - was the fastest growing party in 1855 and the main anti-Democrat party in New England, the mid-Atlantic states and California. Even in the Midwest, Republican success was often dependent on Know Nothings support. The American party's success spread to the slave states. In 1855 it carried Texas, Kentucky and Maryland and provided strong competition to the Democrats in many other Southern states. Southerners supported the party for a variety of reasons. Anti-immigration was an important issue in some areas, especially towns like Baltimore and New Orleans. Many Southerners were as fiercely anti-Catholic as Northerners. But in most Southern states, the American party was essentially the Whig party under a new name. Southern Whigs, who opposed the Democrats, who were committed to preserving the Union, and who recognised that merely continuing as Whigs would be suicidal, had nowhere else to go.

Ironically Know Nothing success in the South was to be one reason for the movement's undoing. In June 1855 a national convention of Know Nothings met at Philadelphia. It was soon clear that the delegates were split over the question of Kansas-Nebraska. Although most Northern delegates hoped to reach a compromise with their Southern counterparts, 53 Northerners withdrew from the convention when it refused to condemn the Kansas-Nebraska Act. Divisions within the American party were not helped by the deteriorating situation in Kansas. The Know Nothings had won massive support in the North in 1854-5 because the order had been able to exploit both anti-slavery and nativist issues. However, by 1856 the American party - if it was to be a national party - had no option but to drop its anti-Kansas-Nebraska position. By so doing, it lost Northern support.

Other factors also damaged the American party. The decline of immigration in the mid-1850s (it fell to under half the level it had been in the early 1850s) resulted in a decline of nativism. The fact that Know Nothing-dominated legislatures often failed to make good their campaign promises did not help the nativist cause: Know Nothing critics were able to claim that the movement actually did nothing. Some Americans disliked the secretive side of the movement: others disliked the bully-boy tactics sometimes employed against immigrants. The very success of the American party helped tarnish its image as an authentic people's party: its growing strength attracted to it many of the 'old guard' politicians - the very people the Know Nothing order had been set up to help purge. This led to widespread disillusionment..

Nevertheless, at the end of 1855 it was far from clear that the American party was on the point of collapse. In the autumn 1855 elections there was no great Republican breakthrough. The Republicans' main success came in Ohio where Salmon Chase became Governor. But Chase only succeeded because he had Know Nothing assistance. Elsewhere - in New York, California, New Hampshire, Rhode Island, Maryland, Delaware, Kentucky and Louisiana - the Know Nothings continued to do well. At the end of 1855 most political observers still assumed that the 1856 presidential election would be between the Know Nothings and the Democrat party.

But events in Congress, which met in December 1855, indicated that the situation might be different. In Congress there was no doubt that the 80 or so Democrats were in a distinct minority. But it was difficult then (and now) to say which Congressmen were Republican and which were Know-Nothing. When the Congressmen had been elected in 1854-5, about two-thirds of the anti-Nebraskan members had been affiliated with the Know Nothings. But since then over a year had elapsed. Probably 105 were anti-Nebraska or Republicans, but 70 of these still had at least nominal connections with the Know Nothings. There were about 50 American party members (of whom 31 came from the South).

If all the nativists had co-operated they would probably have had a majority in the House. But the Know Nothings were split North and South. Through December and January there was a great struggle for the powerful position of the speakership of the House of Representatives. The Know Nothings hoped to use the election as an opportunity to reunite their Northern and Southern factions. But the Republicans finally won the fight when Nathaniel Banks from Massachusetts became speaker on the 133 ballot. Banks had belonged to a Know Nothing lodge, but like many Northerners now sympathised more with the Republicans. His appointment divided Northern and Southern Know Nothings. Moreover, the speakership contest had done much to weld the Republican forces into a more coherent party.

8 The Republican Party in 1856

The Republican party held its first national meeting in Pittsburgh in February 1856. Like all US parties, it was a disparate, heterogeneous coalition. It included abolitionists and Free Soilers (like Charles Sumner); ex-Whigs (like William Seward and Abraham Lincoln); former Democrats (like David Wilmot); and former Know Nothings (like Nathaniel Banks). Inevitably, Republicans held a variety of - often opposed - ideas, which changed over time. Historians, therefore, have different opinions about what the Republican party stood for and why Northerners supported it. Some have argued there was a unifying ideology - but cannot agree precisely what it was: others, are doubtful whether there was ever a central core of beliefs which all Republicans held.

It is far easier to say what Republicans were against than what they were for. Obviously they were against the Democrat party. William Gienapp has persuasively claimed that almost all Republicans were also united in opposition to the 'Slave Power', believing that a Slave Power conspiracy threatened republican liberty, equality and self-government. Far more Republicans, in Gienapp's opinion, were concerned about the Slave Power than they were about slavery itself - or even slavery expansion. Gienapp has pointed out that the notion of a Slave Power conspiracy was far from well defined. Republican leaders never proved the existence of it: nor were they consistent in defining who was actually conspiring. Was it all - or just some - Southern planters? Was it all Southern slaveholders? Was it all Southerners? Republicans also had different views about the nature of the conspiracy. Most thought that, having eradicated the basic rights of Southern whites, the Slave Power aimed, through control of the national government, to stamp out the liberties of Northern whites. Many were convinced it sought to re-establish slavery in the North. There is no doubt that Republican claims and fears were, at best, grossly exaggerated. The planters did not have total power in the South. Nor were they united. Nevertheless, however mistaken and ambiguous, the idea of a Slave Power conspiracy was an article of faith of all Republicans.

Historians disagree about precisely what the Republican position was on slavery and how central that stand was to the party's appeal. Many Republican leaders were certainly concerned about the welfare of black Americans, free and slave. Moral antipathy to slavery was a moving force behind the party. Most leading abolitionists voted Republican and some joined the Republican party. Anti-slavery was, thus, an important part of the Republican ideology. Some Republicans went beyond slavery and supported equal rights for free blacks. Republicans were far more likely to vote against discriminatory laws at state level than Democrats. But by no means all Republicans were committed abolitionists and relatively few believed in black equality. While almost all were opposed to slavery expansion, most were opposed to immediate abolition of slavery in the South and few believed that Congress had the right to interfere with slavery in states in which it already existed. Many feared the consequences of abolition The prospect of thousands of emancipated slaves pouring northwards was not attractive. Concern for the welfare of blacks was not a strong sentiment in the North and Republican strategists were well aware of this. Most Republican leaders, while trying to avoid making racist declarations, believed in white superiority - like the vast majority of Northern voters.

The historian Eric Foner has claimed that the concept of 'free labour' lay at the heart of Republican ideology. Republicans, he thought, shared a desire to protect the free labour system by blocking the expansion of slavery. While extolling the virtues of a free society (which stressed the dignity of labour and encouraged social mobility), they claimed that slavery impoverished the South, especially poor whites. However, most Northern Democrats held similar economic views. It is thus difficult to claim that free labour was the cornerstone of Republican ideology.

Early twentieth century historians like Charles Beard played down the moral side of the sectional struggle, arguing that anti-slavery rhetoric was merely a cloak for sectional economic interests. Beard thought that the Republican party essentially represented the forces of emerging industrial capitalism and that its main concern was the promotion of industrialisation: its supporters wanted a high tariff, a centralised banking system, government aid to internal improvements and a homestead law. Few historians would now accept this thesis. In the 1850s industrialisation does not seem to have been a major concern of most Republican voters, the majority of whom were small farmers. The party itself was divided on many economic issues like the tariff and the national bank, and did not always stress these issues in elections before 1860.

The Republicans were also divided on nativist issues. Some Republican leaders (like Chase) wanted to appeal to both anti-slavery and anti-Catholic forces and reach a compromise with - or steal the clothing of - the Know Nothings. But others, like Seward and Lincoln, wanted no concessions to nativism. Republicans were similarly divided over the issue of temperance.

Perhaps the only thing that can be said with safety is that Republican ideology was multifacetted. It could appeal in different ways to different groups within the party and it gave Northerners of divergent political and social background a basis for collective action. But virtually all Republicans had some things in common: they were committed to the Northern social system; and they believed this - free labour - system was threatened by the Slave Power which was perceived to hold in sway a stagnant Southern society, totally alien to that of the North. The Republican position in early 1856 was still precarious. In a number of state elections in the spring of 1856 the Republican performance was disappointing and the American party continued to do well. Events in Kansas did ensure that the main Republican issue remained in the public eye. But a single event in Congress in May 1856 may have been more important in helping Republican fortunes. This event followed an impassioned speech in the Senate in which the abolitionist Senator Charles Sumner from Massachusetts bitterly attacked the 60 year old Southern Senator Andrew Butler of South Carolina. Incensed by the speech, Congressman Preston Brooks of South Carolina, a relative of Senator Butler, entered the Senate, found Sumner at his desk and proceeded to use his cane to beat the Senator, shattering his cane in the process. (Sumner's supporters claimed his injuries were so severe that he was unable to return to the Senate for over two years: his opponents claimed he was 'milking' his martyrdom for all it was worth.) Gienapp, in particular, has emphasised the importance of the Sumner beating: in his view 'bleeding Sumner' outraged Northerners more than 'bleeding Kansas'. Such was the level of indignation and anger in the North, that 'Almost overnight the entire complexion of the Presidential campaign was transformed'. Here was clear evidence of the Slave Power at work, using brute force to silence free speech.

While Sumner became a Northern martyr, Brooks became a Southern hero. Although he was fined $300 for the assault, Southern Congressmen ensured he was not expelled from Congress. But Brooks resigned anyway, stood for re-election and won easily. Scores of Southerners, approving his action, sent him new canes to replace the one he had broken when beating Sumner and suggested that other Northern Senators would benefit from similar treatment. The South's endorsement of Brooks' action further aided the Republican cause.

9 The 1856 Presidential Election

The Republican party was also helped by developments within the Know Nothing movement. The American party, which held its national convention in February 1856, hoped to heal its sectional breach. Some of the Northern delegates who had walked out in June 1855 returned to the fold. But after a call to repeal the Kansas-Nebraska Act was defeated, 73 Northern delegates left the organisation and formed a splinter 'North American' Party. The official American party, very much a pale imitation of the original Know Nothing order, went on to select ex-President Fillmore as its presidential candidate. This proved to be a serious mistake. More concerned about the preservation of the Union than immigration or Catholicism, Fillmore seemed more an old-fashioned Whig rather than a Know Nothing. Although he was a Northerner, he was known to have pro-Southern sympathies (as President in 1850 he had signed the Fugitive Slave Law) and thus was not the best candidate to win Northern Know Nothing support. North American party members determined not to support him. Instead they planned to meet in June to make their own presidential nomination. Many North Americans hoped that they and the Republicans might be able to select a candidate acceptable to both parties.

The Republicans had a number of potential candidates. These included Samuel Chase and William Seward. Chase, however, seemed too radical on the anti-slavery front while Seward, who had openly denounced the Know Nothings, was unlikely to win nativist support. Republican leaders, therefore, decided that the party's best choice would be a political outsider, John C. Frémont. Born and bred in the South, Frémont had had a colourful career. A Western explorer and mapper, he had crossed the Rocky Mountains five times in the 1840s and 1850s, showing courage and resourcefulness. The 'Pathfinder' was also a national hero: many saw him (wrongly) as the 'Conqueror of California' in 1846. (While he had assumed leadership of some American settlers in California, he had actually achieved very little, except getting in the way of the official USA forces!) Still relatively young (he was 43 in 1856), he had limited political experience. An ex-Know Nothing, he had been a (Democrat!) Senator for California for just 17 days.

A Southern-born, Know Nothing, Democrat Senator, might seem a strange choice for Republican presidential candidate. But this was a time of political flux when many men were moving from party to party. The romance surrounding Frémont's career was likely to make him a popular candidate. His lack of political experience meant he had few enemies. He also had some influential supporters within the Republican party. These included shrewd political operators like Nathaniel Banks, Francis Blair, and Horace Greeley, editor of the influential *New York Tribune*. Frémont's wife Jessica, the gifted daughter of Senator Thomas Hart Benton, was also an asset. (She had far more political ability than her husband.) The fact that Frémont was regarded as a moderate and not closely identified with any particular faction was an additional advantage. Those who knew Frémont well were aware that he was rash, egoistical and lacking in judgement. But these flaws in character could easily be concealed from the electorate.

Confident that Frémont was an excellent candidate, the Republicans' main fear was that the North Americans, whose convention met in New York a few days before their own, might nominate him first. The Republicans might then have no option but to endorse Frémont, if only to avoid splitting the anti-slavery vote. But he would obviously not then be a fully-fledged Republican candidate. Skullduggery on the part of Nathaniel Banks saved the day. Banks allowed his name to be put forward as the North American presidential candidate, ensuring that Frémont was not nominated. Banks intended to withdraw from the contest once Frémont was nominated by the Republicans, leaving the North Americans in the lurch.

The scheme worked to perfection. In June 1856 2,000 Republican delegates met at Philadelphia and Frémont was easily nominated. Banks now withdrew in Frémont's favour and urged North Americans to vote for Frémont. The North Americans had little choice but to endorse the man who was now patently the Republican nominee. The North Americans hope that the Republicans might nominate a North American as Vice President also failed to materialise. At state level, however, Republican parties often made considerable concessions to the North Americans. Some state coalitions even eschewed the name Republican for titles like 'Union' or 'People's' Parties, sometimes dividing the tickets for state offices between Know Nothings and Republicans.

The Republican platform was reasonably radical. It made clear the party's anti-slavery principles. Congress, it declared, had 'both the right and the imperative duty ... to prohibit in the Territories those twin relics of barbarism - Polygamy and Slavery'. (The polygamy reference was an unequivocal - and certainly popular - attack on Mormon practices in Utah.) The platform also condemned the violation of the rights of free state Kansanians and supported the notion of a Pacific railroad, by the most practical (i.e. Northern) route. In most respects, however, the platform was more a guideline of principle than a list of specific actions. It made no reference to how the Republicans would deal with the Fugitive Slave Law. It said nothing about slavery in the District of Columbia. It also said little about nativist issues. But at least the Republican slogan was clear cut and one of which today's spin-doctors would be proud: 'Free Soil, Free Labour, Free Men, Frémont'

The Democrats, facing divisions between their Northern and Southern wings, could at least agree that Pierce was so unpopular that he faced almost certain defeat. Douglas, the most dynamic and talented Democrat, was tarnished (in the North) by events in Kansas and was unpopular with many leading Democrats who disliked him personally. In the end Douglas agreed to withdraw his name in the interests of the party, and the Democrats came up with a compromise candidate, James Buchanan. Although 64 years old and totally lacking in charisma, Buchanan seemed 'safe'. He had spent four decades in public service, served in both the House and Senate, and been American minister in Russia and Britain. The fact that he had been abroad meant that he was unconnected with the unpopular Democrat policies of 1854-6. A Northerner, he was nevertheless acceptable to the South. Given that his native state was Pennsylvania, which most experts regarded as the key 'battle-ground' state, he was probably the Democrats' strongest candidate. Breckinridge, a Douglas supporter, became the Democrats' Vice Presidential candidate. The Democratic platform upheld the 1850 Compromise, endorsed popular sovereignty and supported the Union.

The 1856 campaign, with events in Kansas as a backdrop, generated great excitement. In the North, the contest was essentially between Buchanan and Frémont. In the South, it was between Buchanan and

Fillmore. For the first time since 1849-50 there was widespread fear for the safety of the Union. The Republican party had no base or support in the South. If Frémont won, it was quite conceivable that many Southern states would secede from the Union. Senator Toombs of Georgia had no doubts: 'The election of Frémont', he declared, 'would be the end of the Union and ought to be'.

In the North, the Republicans formed Wide Awake clubs - marching societies whose members held mass torchlight parades. (Many of the original Know Nothing lodges had been called 'Wide Awakes' and many ex-Know Nothings now marched in Republican parades.) Republicans stressed the fact that Frémont was young and vibrant whereas Buchanan was portrayed as an old fogey and a lackey of the South. The Democrat party, however, was still a major force. Northern Democrats, claiming that they stood for stability and peace, appealed to ex-Whig moderates. (The sons of Henry Clay and Daniel Webster announced their support of Buchanan on the grounds that he was the Unionist candidate.) Stressing their long-time defence of religious and ethnic minorities, Democrats attacked the Republicans for being intolerant bigots and self-righteous 'do-gooders'. Northern Democrats also played the racial 'card', claiming that the Republicans were 'amalgamationists' and rabid abolitionists who aimed to elevate the African race to complete equality. 'The white race or the Negro race' became a key issue in some Northern states.

American party attacks on Frémont were also telling. During the campaign, he was accused of being illegitimate (which was true) and for being a Catholic (which was false). The Catholic charge caused Frémont and the Republicans great difficulty because there seemed plenty of circumstantial evidence to substantiate it. Frémont's father had been a French Catholic. Frémont, himself, had been married by a Catholic priest. His adopted daughter had attended a Catholic school. Moreover several of Frémont's 'friends' testified that he remained Catholic. Thousands of Northerners, suspecting that Frémont was a closet Catholic, determined not to vote Republican.

83 per cent of the electorate voted in the November 1856 election. Fillmore won 871,731 votes (21.6 per cent of the total but only 13 per cent of the vote in the free states) and 8 electoral college votes. Frémont won 1,340,537 votes (33.1 per cent in total: 45 per cent of the Northern vote - but only 1,196 votes in the South) and won 114 electoral college votes. Buchanan, with 1,832,955 votes (45.3 per cent of the total) and 174 electoral votes, won the election and became President.

Fillmore trailed Buchanan by only 479,000 to 609,000 votes in the South as a whole. With the change of a few thousand voters in Kentucky, Louisiana and Tennessee, he would have carried these states and thrown the election into the House of Representatives - where he stood a chance of victory. As it was, Buchanan won every Southern state (except Maryland), plus Pennsylvania, New Jersey, Indiana, Illinois and

California. Frémont won the rest of the free states. The Republicans were particularly successful in New England and in areas dominated by ex-New Englanders. Skilled workers and small farmers - native-born and Protestant - were the mainstay of the party.

The Democrats had cause for celebration. They had seen off the Fillmore challenge in the South and succeeded in retaining their traditional supporters - the Catholics and the Midwestern farmers - in the North. Northern Democrats actually increased the number of seats they held in the House to 53 - although they were still outnumbered by 75 Southern Democrats and 92 Republicans. Some Republicans were disappointed by the results. However, when they had time to consider what had happened, they too had cause for optimism. In many ways, what was remarkable in 1856 was not that Frémont lost but that he had done so well. From 1854 the Republicans and Know Nothings had battled for control of the anti-Democrat forces in the North. The 1856 election showed that the Republicans had destroyed the Northern Know Nothings, a remarkable performance given the situation in the spring of 1856. The election indicated that Northerners perceived the Slave Power to be a greater threat than the Catholic Church. Moreover, the Republicans had actually come close to capturing the presidency. If the party had carried Pennsylvania and Illinois, Frémont would have become President. Party leaders, confident they could bring the remaining anti-Democrat groups in the North into the Republican coalition, realised they stood an excellent chance of victory in 1860.

10 Conclusion

The political crisis of the mid-1850s had fundamentally reshaped the nature of party competition. The national two party system of Whigs and Democrats had collapsed. In its place by 1856 was a sectional Northern Republican party and a Democrat party, which, although national, was dominated by the South. Each section by 1856 viewed the other as bent on usurping the government and perverting the traditional basis of society. Sectional antagonism by itself had not caused the voter realignment, nor the death of the Whig party. The Know Nothings' meteoric rise and fall from 1853 to 1856 played a vital transitional role. Know Nothingism had emerged initially as a grass roots protest movement against the unresponsiveness of the established parties to the felt needs of the electorate. It was an important halfway house to new affiliations. Thousands of ex-Democrat voters, who could probably never have brought themselves to support the Whigs, moved through the Know Nothings to the Republican party. Northern voter realignment, therefore, worked against the Democrat party as well as against the Whigs.

Although optimistic Republican pundits were soon predicting victory in 1860, that victory was far from certain. The Democrat vote in the

North had declined but it had not disappeared. The ferocity of both the Know Nothings and the Republican assaults on Catholics, immigrants and 'wets' ensured that these targets had a new appreciation of the Democrat party. Throughout the 1850s, the Democrats continued to win at least 40 per cent of the Northern vote. (They won 44 per cent in 1856). Nor in 1856 was there any guarantee that Northerners would continue to vote Republican. The Republican party was far from united. It was possible that it would collapse as quickly as it had risen. It might prove impossible for Republicans to sustain the notion of a Slave Power conspiracy. If Buchanan managed to solve the situation in Kansas, the Republicans would be left without a major issue on which to campaign. Buchanan's presidency would thus be crucial in determining the outcome of the 1860 presidential election.

Making notes on *'The Rise of the Republican Party'*

Your notes should help you to understand the two main issues dealt with in this chapter:
1   Why did the second party system collapse?
2   Why did the Republicans emerge as the main rival of the Democrats in the 1856 presidential election?
However, your notes also need to provide an answer to a number of subsidiary questions - which go some way to explaining the two main issues above:
3   Why did Douglas introduce the Kansas-Nebraska bill?
4   Why was the Kansas-Nebraska Act important?
5   Why did the Know Nothing movement rise and fall?
6   What was the main ideology of the Republican party?

Answering essay questions on *'The Rise of the Republican Party'*

Questions on this topic are likely to echo the questions posed in the 'notes' section above. Consider the following:

1   'The Kansas-Nebraska Act led to the collapse of the Whig party and the rise of the Republican party'. Do you agree?
2   'For most of the period from 1854-6 Northern public opinion was more concerned with nativism than slavery expansion.' Discuss.

Quotes in essay questions worry many students. Some assume they have to agree with them! (You don't!) Do you agree with the quote in question 1? Brainstorm what points you might be making for and against the quote. Hopefully you will be saying that it contains an element of truth: the Kansas-Nebraska Act did not help the Whig cause and did lead to the establishment of various anti-Nebraska parties - including the

Republican party. However, you will also (hopefully) be saying that the quote, as it stands, is far too simplistic. The Kansas-Nebraska Act was just one factor leading to the decline of the Whig party: there were many others. Make a rough plan of the main seven or eight paragraphs of the essay. What would your conclusion be?

Question 2 is more difficult. Many students would rush into it and write everything they know about the period 1854-6, in the process unintentionally doing almost everything in their power to avoid answering the question set. That is the worst possible thing to do. You must first consider the quote. To what extent do you agree with it? There were no opinion polls in the mid-1850s but there were a considerable number of elections at national, state and local level. These give us some indication of the views of the Northern electorate. Unfortunately, voters in different states voted differently at different times. Many in the Midwest do seem to have regarded slavery expansion as THE crucial issue. But the same does not seem to have been true elsewhere - at least not until the spring and summer of 1856. To further complicate matters, many (and perhaps most) Northerners supported politicians who were anti-immigrant and anti-Slave Power at one and the same time! Nativism and slavery expansion were not exclusive and necessarily opposing issues. The points just made should help you write an introduction. The rest is up to you. Again, draw up a rough plan, with about seven or eight main paragraphs. Then write a conclusion of about seven or eight sentences.

Source-based questions on *'The Rise of the Republican Party'*

1 Opposition to the Kansas-Nebraska Bill
Read the extract from 'The Appeal of the Independent Democrats' on page 73 and the Theodore Parker extract on page3 73-74. Answer the following questions:
a) What are the main arguments put forward against the Kansas-Nebraka Bill in the 'Appeal'? (4 marks)
b) What are the main arguments against the bill in the Theodore Parker extract? (3 marks)
c) Comment on the tone of the 'Appeal'? (4 marks)
d) What arguments might Douglas have made in response to these Northern criticisms of his bill? (4 marks)

2 The Know Nothings
Read the account of the Detroit judge on page 79 and the comment from Abraham Lincoln on page 80. Answer the following questions:
a) Why, according to the judge, was the USA in danger? (4 marks)
b) Why, according to Lincoln, was the USA in danger? (4 marks)
c) The judge implies there was a Papal conspiracy. But no evidence of

such a conspiracy has ever been found. Does this mean that the source is of no use to historians? (3 marks)

d) Might Lincoln and the judge have had anything in common? (4 marks)

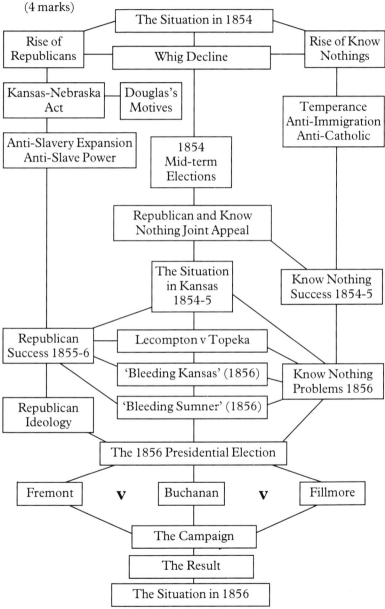

Summary - The Rise of the Republican Party

CHAPTER 6

The Presidency of James Buchanan

1 Introduction

At the start of 1857 many Americans, not least the new President James Buchanan, were reasonably optimistic about the future. The Democrat election success in 1856 had prevented a major schism. If the problem of Kansas could be quickly solved, then sectional tension was likely to ease. No other territory, at least in the immediate future, was likely to be so contentious. Once Kansas was out of the way there was a strong possibility that the Republican party, which had existed for little more than two years, might go into rapid decline. Buchanan's position seemed strong. As a new President, he was not linked to any of the mistakes of the recent past. Moreover, both Houses of Congress and the Supreme Court were securely in the hands of the Democrat party.

This was the situation at the start of 1857. The historian Kenneth Stampp has contended that by the end of 1857 both North and South had probably reached 'the political point of no return'. The events of 1857, according to Stampp, proved to be a decisive factor in preventing a peaceful resolution to sectional strife. Slavery - or rather slavery expansion - lay at the heart of the sectional animosity. But Buchanan, in Stampp's view, must shoulder much of the blame for pursuing policies which alienated Northerners and pushed many of them firmly into the Republican camp. Those same policies also contributed to the fragmentation of the Democrat party, the last important national institution which had ties binding North and South. Other historians have similarly blamed Buchanan. Alan Nevins considered Buchanan's role in 1857-8 as 'one of the significant failures of American statesmanship'. Is this fair? Should Buchanan be held seriously responsible for the outbreak of Civil War?

2 James Buchanan

In 1857 Buchanan seemed likely to be a safe, if not a dynamic, President. Born in 1791 in Pennsylvania, he had risen from poverty to both wealth and fame. In 1857 he was a respected elder statesman, with as much political experience as almost anyone in the USA. A loyal Democrat, he had served for over 40 years - in both the House and Senate, in the Cabinet (as Secretary of State), and as American minister in Russia and Britain. Within months, however, many contemporaries had come to the conclusion that he was pedestrian, pliable, reticent and lacking in personal charm. Historians have tended to echo this verdict. Alan Nevins said: 'He never made a witty remark, never wrote a memorable sentence, and never showed a touch of distinction. Above all (and this was the source of his irresolution) he had no strong conviction'.

A 'doughface' (a Northerner with Southern principles), Buchanan despised abolitionists and thought that maintaining the Union was far more important than interfering with slavery. His choice of cabinet indicated his pro-Southern leanings. No less than four of his cabinet members were slaveowners. By and large, he appointed a 'yes' cabinet: that is, one that was unlikely to fall out. In consequence, he did not appoint Douglas (who he did not personally like or trust) and also ignored his cabinet recommendations. Douglas, who had campaigned vigorously on Buchanan's behalf, was left suspicious and disgruntled. Buchanan needed the support of the South. Nearly two-thirds of the electoral votes that had made him President came from the slave states. The Democrat majority in both Houses was dominated by Southerners. Alienating the South was likely to have disastrous consequences. But Buchanan also needed to increase the Democrat appeal to Northern voters. Not to do so would be to convince many Northerners that he, like Presidents Fillmore and Pierce before him, was simply a tool of the Slave Power. The fact that Douglas was ignored and that Northerners were under-represented on Buchanan's cabinet were thus serious blunders.

3 The Dred Scott Case

Buchanan had to face a major problem at the very start of his presidency. This problem was the Dred Scott case. Dred Scott was a slave. For much of his life he had been owned by an army surgeon whom he had accompanied first to the free state of Illinois, then to the Wisconsin territory, before finally returning to Missouri. On the surgeon's death in 1843 Scott became the property of one of the surgeon's relations. Three years later, Scott, with the help of local anti-slavery lawyers, went before the Missouri courts, claiming he was free on the grounds that he had resided both in a free state and a free territory. The Scott case proved to be long and drawn out. When the Missouri Supreme Court finally voted against Scott, his lawyers took his case to the Federal courts. Eventually it reached the Supreme Court. There were two main questions. Was Scott a citizen with the right to sue in Federal courts? And was he free as a result of having lived in the Wisconsin territory, where slavery had been outlawed by the Missouri Compromise? By March 1857 the Supreme Court judges, having heard the case articulated by some of the best legal brains in the country, were ready to give judgement. They were well aware of the interest in the case and its political dimensions.

On 6 March 1857 Buchanan delivered his inaugural address. In his speech he referred to the pending Scott judgement. He claimed he knew nothing of the Court's decision (which was not quite true) but said he was confident that the Court would provide a 'final settlement' to the dispute over slavery in the territories. He was prepared to 'cheerfully submit' to the verdict of the Court and urged all good citizens to do likewise. Two days later the Supreme Court's decision was made public. The Court was composed of nine Justices: five were Southerners; four were Northerners. The Chief Justice was Roger Taney. Now aged 79, he had been appointed to the Supreme Court in 1835 and had sworn in seven Presidents. A Catholic from a Maryland planter family, he had actually liberated his own slaves. But Taney was committed to the Southern way of life and to Southern values. Under his leadership the Court decided to make a comprehensive ruling covering all aspects of the Scott case. It had no need to do so. It could - and perhaps should - have said that Scott's status was determined by the law of Missouri. The Court's decision to issue a major statement was a victory for the judges who wanted to settle the uncertainty about slavery in the territories and issue an emphatic pro-Southern verdict.

The Court decided that Scott could not sue for his freedom. Black Americans, it contended, had no rights which white men were bound to respect. It claimed that at the time of the framing of the Constitution, blacks were regarded as inferior. In consequence, neither slaves nor their descendents could or should have the rights of white citizens. Scott's sojourn in a Federal territory did not make him free. The Court declared that the 1820 Missouri Compromise ban on slavery in territories north of 36°.30 was illegal. All American citizens had the right to take their 'property' into the territories. These decisions were accepted by seven of the Justices. However, two Northern Justices, Curtis and McLean, dissented from the majority view and wrote a minority report, justifying their opposition. This contended first that the Constitution did not deny citizenship to blacks; second that the Constitution gave Congress the power to govern the territories; and third that the Missouri Compromise was constitutional and valid.

Most Northerners were horrified at the majority decision. Some thought it presaged a move by Southerners to expand slavery into the free states. At the very least, it seemed further evidence of the Slave Power at work. The fact that Taney had been seen whispering with Buchanan on the day of his inauguration seemed further proof of that conspiracy. Republican leaders claimed that the whispered conversation proved that Buchanan had been well aware of what the Supreme Court's decision was when he asked Americans to accept it. In the fevered minds of many Republicans, the President, the Supreme Court and the Democrat party, were all involved in the great conspiracy against the North. The Northern press launched a fierce onslaught on the Supreme Court and some editors talked openly of defying the law.

In reality, the Dred Scott judgement was easier to denounce than defy. Probably no other major judicial decision in American history has practically affected the daily lives of so few people as the Dred Scott judgement. In part, it simply annulled a law which had already been repealed by the Kansas-Nebraska Act. The Supreme Court's decision even had little effect on Scott. Thanks to Northern sympathisers, he soon purchased his freedom and died in obscurity in September 1858.

Nevertheless, the Dred Scott outcome was important. Rather than settling the uncertainty about slavery in the territories, as Buchanan had hoped, the decision helped provoke further sectional antagonism. As far as Northerners were concerned, it could be seen as an attempt to outlaw the Republican party, which was committed to the exclusion of slavery from the territories. Moreover, the judgement even undermined the Northern Democrat version of popular sovereignty - that territorial legislatures could prohibit slavery if they chose. Douglas soon got round this potential embarrassment by arguing that slaves could be taken into any territory but it was up to the people in the territory to decide whether to pass the appropriate police regulations necessary to maintain slavery. Douglas was, thus, able to claim that slavery would not be forced upon an unwilling majority in any territory.

Republicans made every effort to gain political capital from the Dred Scott decision. But they had less success than they had hoped. The Democrats continued to do well in the spring and summer elections of 1857, particularly in the key states of Pennsylvania and New York..

4 The Panic of 1857

Buchanan soon had to face another problem not of his own making. From 1848 to 1856 the United States had enjoyed a great economic boom. But in 1857 depression set in. The 'Panic of 1857' , which had both domestic and foreign roots, resulted in the collapse of hundreds of American companies and mass Northern unemployment. Buchanan, his cabinet and most Democrats in Congress believed the Federal government should not involve itself in economic matters. Such interference, they thought, would damage both the country and individuals. If the government left alone, the economy would ultimately right itself.

Inevitably Buchanan and the Democrats were blamed for their seeming indifference to the plight of Northern industry and labour. Republican economic proposals - internal improvement measures; a Homestead Act giving free public land to Western settlers; and higher protective tariffs - were blocked by Democrats in Congress. The depression had little effect in the South where cotton prices remained high. Southerners claimed that this proved the strength of their system. Fortunately the depression was relatively short-lived. By 1859 the recovery was almost complete. Nevertheless, the depression had important political effects in the 1858 mid-term elections. So too did events in Kansas.

5 Problems in Kansas

In Kansas, in the spring of 1857, Buchanan faced a situation which seemed to offer more in the way of hope than despair. By the end of 1856 governor Geary had restored order in the territory. It was obvious to Geary, and to other independent observers, that free-staters now had a clear majority in Kansas. Buchanan had announced at his inauguration that he was committed to popular sovereignty. Most Democrats supported this policy. Even Southern Democrats were not opposed to fair elections in Kansas. All that Buchanan needed to do, therefore, was ensure that the will of the majority prevailed.

At the start of 1857 there were still two governments in Kansas - the official pro-slave Lecompton government and the unofficial free state government at Topeka. Both had dubious credentials. Geary who had arrived in Kansas heartily despising abolitionists, had by the start of 1857 turned against the pro-slavery party. Threatened with assassination by pro-slavers, he resigned in March 1857, warning Buchanan that he should not support the pro-slavers. It seemed that Buchanan would heed this advice. He now appointed Robert Walker in Geary's place. Walker, an experienced Mississippi politician, was committed to popular sovereignty and was given firm assurances from Buchanan that he and his cabinet would support fair elections.

Arriving in Kansas in May, Walker realised almost immediately that the majority of people in the territory opposed slavery. But he also believed that most settlers supported the Democrat party. Walker decided, in consequence, that his aim should be to bring Kansas into the Union as a free, Democrat-voting state similar to California, Oregon and Minnesota. Walker's aim obviously made sense. Realising the aim, however, was never likely to be easy given the ill-feeling that existed between pro-slavers and free-staters. In February 1857 the Lecompton pro-slavery government had authorised the election (in June) of a constitutional convention which would meet in September to draw up a constitution which would set the territory on the road to statehood. Free-staters, suspecting (quite understandably) that any election organised by the pro-slavers would be rigged, were reluctant to get involved. Walker was too late arriving in Kansas to change the election procedure. He did his best to urge the free-state men to participate in the election but they refused. In the event only 2,200 of the registered 9,000 people entitled to vote did so. The result was that the pro-slavers, who alone canvassed the election returns, won all the seats in the convention.

Walker now had problems. Pro-slavers, angry at Walker's free-state sympathies, protested to Washington. Meanwhile Walker had to deal with the Lecompton constitutional convention. While its election had made a mockery of popular sovereignty, the convention had been elected in a legal manner. This had raised the expectations of Southerners. Many - who previously had thought that Kansas would inevitably become a free state - now realised that the creation of a new slave state was a real possibility. The Lecompton convention, which met in September 1857, did not remain long in session because new elections - this time for a new territorial Kansas legislature - were in the offing. These elections were held in October. By now Walker had managed to convince the free-staters that they should take part, assuring them that he would overseer procedures and do all he could to see that the elections (organised by the pro-slavers) were fairly conducted. Walker's vigilance ensured that few Missourians crossed into Kansas to vote. Not withstanding this, the pro-slavers still won a majority. Free-staters immediately charged the pro-slavers with massive fraudulence. The charges were easily confirmed. Large numbers of fictitious people had been recorded as voting for the pro-slavers. One village, for example, with 30 eligible voters returned more than 1,600 pro-slavery votes. Walker over-turned enough fraudulent election results to give the free-staters a majority in the Kansas legislature.

The constitutional convention was now the last refuge of the pro-slavery minority. Few thought that this body seriously represented majority opinion in Kansas. Nevertheless the convention drafted a pro-slavery constitution - the so-called Lecompton constitution - in which slave property was 'inviolable'. The convention had assured Walker that it would give Kansas voters a choice to accept or reject the proposed constitution. But instead it offered something of a spurious choice: voters had to accept the pro-slavery constitution as it was; or accept another constitution which prohibited the future importation of slaves into Kansas but still guaranteed the rights of those slaveholders already in Kansas. Mass meetings throughout Kansas repudiated the constitution and pledged themselves to have nothing to do with the coming referendum. Walker denounced the convention's actions as a 'vile fraud' and urged Buchanan to repudiate the proposed Lecompton constitution.

Buchanan faced something of a dilemma. Until now, he had supported Walker rather better than Pierce had supported Reeder, Shannon or Geary. But most of his cabinet objected to Walker. Moreover, if he refused to support the Lecompton convention he would probably alienate the Southern wing of the Democrat party. Some influential Southerners now insisted on making the Lecompton constitution a test of the South's ability to find equality within the Union. The ultimatum - 'Lecompton or disunion' - rang out in Southern legislatures and in Southern newspapers. Buchanan knew he could not afford to lose Southern support. However, it seems that he decided to support the actions of the Lecompton convention, not so much because he was browbeaten by his Southern advisers or feared a Southern rebellion, but more because he thought it to be the judicious and patriotic thing to do. He seems to have genuinely believed that the anti-slavery forces were to blame for all the troubles in Kansas.

Walker, his health failing, left Kansas in November. In Washington, he met Buchanan and his cabinet and insisted that the Lecompton constitution did not fulfil the promise of popular sovereignty. He failed to change Buchanan's mind. In December, therefore, Walker resigned as governor declaring he had been let down by the President. That same month Kansas voted on the Lecompton constitution. In fact, most of the Kansas electorate did not vote: free-staters abstained in protest. The 'official' (i.e. fraudulent pro-slave) returns showed 6,143 for the Lecompton constitution with slavery and 569 for it without slavery. None of this had any effect on Buchanan. In his annual message to Congress, he endorsed the actions of the Lecompton convention, claiming that it had been legally elected and that the question of slavery had been 'fairly and explicitly referred to the people'.

Buchanan's decision to support the actions of the Lecompton convention was a colossal blunder. By the end of 1857 everyone knew that the majority of Kansanians were opposed to slavery. Even some Southerners were embarrassed by the fraud perpetrated by the pro-slavers in Kansas. Had Buchanan accepted Walker's advice, he was unlikely to have lost much Southern support. By accepting the Lecompton constitution, he alienated the North and gave the Republican party massive political ammunition. Here was more proof of the Slave Power conspiracy at work. But even more important, by supporting the 'Lecompton swindle', he enraged Northern Democrats - not least Stephen Douglas - who were committed to supporting popular sovereignty. Douglas, fully briefed by Walker, met Buchanan privately. He urged him not to support Lecompton and threatened to oppose him if he did. Douglas's threat had no effect.

Douglas was as good as his word. As far as he was concerned the issue of popular sovereignty was more important than party unity. In an impassioned speech in the Senate, Douglas attacked both Buchanan and the Lecompton constitution. Southern Democrats immediately denounced Douglas as a traitor. The Democrat party, like almost every other institution in America, was now split North and South.

In January 1858 there was another referendum in Kansas, called by the free-state dominated territorial legislature. This time it was the turn of the pro-slavers to abstain. 10,226 voted against the Lecompton constitution, 138 voted for it with slavery and 24 voted for it without slavery. This vote gave Buchanan a strong excuse to change his mind. General Denver, the new Kansas governor, also advised him to change policy. But Buchanan still refused to do so.

A titanic Congressional contest with Douglas followed, now siding with the Republicans, leading the opposition to Buchanan. Using all the powers of patronage at his disposal, Buchanan tried to ensure that Northern Democrats voted for the Lecompton constitution. Some Northern Democrats were influenced by both bribes and threats. But others, committed to popular sovereignty, aware of the strength of feeling in the North, and fearing defeat in the 1858 mid-term elections, supported Douglas who fought his corner with great resource and passion. Republicans were delighted at the turn of events. The Democrat party was disintegrating before their very eyes. As Buchanan expected, the Senate passed the Lecompton constitution (by 33 to 25 votes). The real battle was in the House. Fierce sectional hatred was expressed in the debates and fist-fights broke out among Congressmen. Despite all the patronage pressure, enough Northern Democrats stuck to their guns and supported Douglas's position to ensure that the Lecompton constitution was defeated by 120 votes to 112.

Buchanan finally recognised that he had gambled and lost. He accepted that the people of Kansas should vote again on the constitution. If they approved the Lecompton constitution, Kansas would be immediately admitted into the Union as a slave state. If they rejected it, Kansas would be entitled to draw up a new constitution but would not be allowed to re-apply for statehood until its population had reached 90,000. The new elections took place in August 1858. Conducted as fairly as possible, they resulted in an impressive free state victory: 11,300 voted against the Lecompton constitution while only 1,788 voted for it. Kansas now set about drawing up a new free state constitution (which excluded blacks!). It finally joined the Union in January 1861 as a free state.

Buchanan had blundered. Had he supported honest elections in Kansas, to which he was supposedly committed, the repercussions in the South would probably have been minimal. Instead his Kansas policy had led to increased sectional strife. The Republicans could maintain their charge that an aggressive Slave Power stalked the land. Moreover, Buchanan had succeeded in dividing his party.

6 The 1858 Congressional Elections

The 1858 mid-term elections came at a bad time for the Democrats. The party was split and Douglas was regarded as a traitor by Buchanan and most Southern Democrats. Such was the hostility between Buchanan and Douglas that the President continued to use his powers of patronage to remove from office all Douglas's supporters, further exacerbating tension within the Democrat party. Douglas himself had to stand for re-election in Illinois in 1858. National attention, therefore, inevitably focused on the Illinois campaign. Moreover, Illinois was important politically. The fourth largest state in the Union, it usually voted Democrat but was felt to be winnable by the Republicans. Its voters could well determine the outcome of the 1860 presidential election. The Buchanan wing of the Democrat party determined to run its own candidate against Douglas. Douglas, however, was more concerned with the Republican challenge. In 1858 some leading Republicans considered uniting behind Douglas in a defiant show of unity against Buchanan. But most Illinois Republicans, unable to forgive Douglas for earlier actions, determined to put forward their own candidate to run against him. The man they chose was Abraham Lincoln.

Lincoln in many ways epitomised the American dream. Born in 1809 in a log cabin in Kentucky, he had little formal schooling. But able and ambitious, he read voraciously and was determined to escape from farming which he hated. He moved to Illinois in 1831 and over the next few years experienced a host of jobs - store clerk, postmaster, surveyor and newspaper subscription agent. In 1832 he volunteered to fight against hostile Native Americans in the Black Hawk war. He was elected captain of militia - his first election triumph - but saw no action. In 1834 he won the first of four terms as an Illinois state legislator. A loyal Whig (his hero was Henry Clay), politics became his passion. In 1837 he moved to the Illinois state capital of Springfield and became a lawyer. In 1842 he married Mary Todd, daughter of a Kentucky slaveholder. His chief political success came in 1846 when he was elected to the House of Representatives. Sitting as a Whig Congressman from 1847 to 1849, his main claim to fame was his opposition to the Mexican War. Defeated in the 1848 election, he returned to Springfield, resumed his successful law practice and for a few years took less interest in politics.

The Kansas-Nebraska Act brought him actively back into the political field. He hoped at first that the Act, which he described as a 'great moral wrong and injustice', would bring new life to the Whigs. Although he had excellent contacts with Republican leaders, he did not officially join the Republican party until 1856. But once committed, he threw himself into the Republican cause with vigour. Previously, his main political concern had been economic matters - particularly Federal support for internal improvements. Now he rearranged his priorities and his speeches became more anti-slavery and anti-Slave Power.

Lincoln was complex and enigmatic. On the one hand he was a calculating politician - often non-committal and evasive. On the other, he was a humane, witty man who never seemed to worry much about his own bruised ego and whose judgement was rarely affected by hurt pride. Although he had not much of a national reputation in 1858, he was well-known in Illinois, both as a lawyer and as a politician. Douglas, who had debated with him on several previous occasions, respected his ability, commenting: 'I shall have my hands full. He is the strong man of the party - full of wit, facts, dates - and the best stump speaker with his droll ways and dry jokes, in the West. He is as honest as he is shrewd'.

Lincoln had always been opposed to slavery, believing it to be both immoral and against the Declaration of Independence's assertion that 'all men are created equal'. But realising that slavery could be a divisive issue, he had kept quiet on the subject for much of the 1840s and early 1850s. While opposing slavery in principle, he had been prepared to tolerate it in practice and had often been critical of abolitionists. He had shown no personal animosity towards Southern slaveowners: indeed he had married one! However, now that he was running against Douglas, he determined to remind Illinois voters of the gulf separating him from his opponent. In his acceptance speech, delivered to the Republican state convention in Springfield on 16 June 1858, he said:

1 A House divided against itself cannot stand. I believe this government cannot endure permanently half slave and half free. I do not expect the Union to be dissolved - I do not expect the house to fall - but I do expect it will cease to be divided. It will become all
5 one thing or all the other. Either the opponents of slavery will arrest the further spread of it, and place it where the public mind shall rest in the belief that it is in the course of ultimate extinction; or its advocates will push it forward till it shall become alike lawful in all the states, old as well as new - north as well as south. Have we no
10 tendency to the latter condition? Let anyone who doubts, carefully contemplate that now almost complete legal combination - piece of machinery so to speak - compounded of the Nebraska doctrine and the Dred Scott decision. Let him consider not only what work the machinery is adapted to do, and how well adapted, but also, let
15 him study the history of its construction, and trace, if he can, or rather fail, if he can, to trace the evidence of design, and concert of action, among its chief bosses from the beginning.

This was perhaps the most important statement of Lincoln's career and set the agenda for the coming debates with Douglas. Lincoln made it perfectly clear that he supported the 'ultimate extinction' of slavery. But he did not spell out how - or precisely when - slavery would become extinct. Like many Republicans, he hoped that if slavery was prevented from expanding, it would ultimately wither and die. He hoped, as well, that Southerners might come to see the error of their ways and that they would end the institution by direct state action. Meanwhile, the North must stand firm against the machinations of the Slave Power.

Douglas, fighting for his political survival, launched his campaign with a spirited defence of popular sovereignty and a proud assertion of his crucial role in securing the defeat of the Lecompton fraud. He attracted large crowds wherever he went. Lincoln's strategy, at first, was to follow him round Illinois, speaking in the same town a day or two after the 'Little Giant' had spoken. But, then he challenged Douglas to a series of open-air debates. Douglas, fearing that he would be charged with cowardice if he refused, agreed to meet for debates in seven of Illinois' nine Congressional districts. (The two men had already spoken in Chicago and Springfield).

The Lincoln-Douglas debates have become part of American political folk lore. They ran from August to October and drew large crowds. Visually the two men were a strange pair: Lincoln, a gawky 6 feet 4 inches tall: Douglas a foot shorter. Both were gifted speakers.

Douglas had a melodious voice and spoke rapidly but also fluently. Lincoln's delivery, marked by his Kentucky twang, was harsher but he was more humourous. As the two men spoke, there were constant interruptions - heckling and cheering. Precisely what was said remains something of a mystery. The newspaper reports of the speeches were polished - or deliberately distorted - by partisan transcribers and newspaper editors. Given the editorial sanitising process, it may well be that the level of rhetoric was not as majestic as folk lore suggests.

The seven debates were only a fraction of each candidate's overall effort. Lincoln made at least 60 other speeches - and Douglas claimed to have made 130. But the face-to-face debates captured the public's imagination. They were confined almost exclusively to three topics - race, slavery and slavery expansion. The two men had been arguing the nuances of their respective positions for years so little was said that was new or unexpected. The Illinois voters, themselves, were also familiar with both the messages and the messengers.

The following extract, from Douglas's opening speech at the first debate on 21 August, is a good indication of Douglas's views and style:

1 Mr Lincoln here says that our government cannot endure permanently in the same condition in which it was made by its framers. It was made divided into free States and slave States. Mr Lincoln says it has existed for near eighty years thus divided; but he
5 tells you that it cannot endure permanently on the same principle and in the same conditions relatively in which your fathers made it ... Why can't it exist upon the same principles upon which our fathers made it? Our fathers knew when they made this government that in a country as wide and broad as this - with such
10 a variety of climate, of interests, of productions as this - that the people necessarily required different local laws and local institutions in certain localities from those in other localities. Hence, they provided that each State should retain its own Legislature and its own sovereignty, with the full and complete
15 power to do as it pleased within its own limits in all that was local and not national. [Applause] One of the reserved rights of the States was that of regulating the relations between master and slave
   ...
   We are told by Lincoln that he is utterly opposed to the Dred
20 Scott decision and will not submit to it, for the reason, as he says, that it deprives the negro of the rights and privileges of citizens ... Now I ask you, are you in favour of conferring upon the negro the rights and privileges of citizenship? [Cries of 'No, no'] Do you desire to strike out of our State Constitution that clause which
25 keeps slaves and free negroes out of the State, and allow free negro to flow in ['never'] and cover our prairies with his settlements? Do you desire to turn this beautiful State into a free negro colony ['no,

no'], in order that when Missouri shall abolish slavery, she can send us these emancipated slaves to become citizens and voters on
30 an equality with you? ['Never, no'] If you desire negro citizenship - if you desire them to come into the State and stay with white men - if you desire to let them vote on an equality with yourselves - if you desire to make them eligible to office - to have them serve on juries and judge of your rights - then go with Mr Lincoln and the Black
35 Republicans in favour of negro citizenship. ['Never, never'] For one, I am opposed to negro citizenship in any form. [Cheers] I believe this government was made on the white basis. I believe it was made by white men for the benefit of white men and their posterity forever, and I am in favour of confining the citizenship to
40 white men - men of European birth and European descent, instead of conferring it upon Negroes and Indians, and other inferior races ... I believe that this new doctrine preached by Mr Lincoln and this Abolition party would dissolve the Union. They try to array all the Northern States in one body against the South, inviting a sectional
45 war of the free States against the slave States.

Given the racist sentiment in Illinois, Lincoln knew he was on difficult ground on the race issue. Douglas was happy to state - with brutal frankness - that he considered blacks to be inferior to whites. Lincoln had some sympathy for this view. In the fourth debate, Lincoln said:

1 I am not, nor ever have been in favour of bringing about in any way the social and political equality of the white and black races, - that I am not nor ever have been in favour of making voters or jurors of negroes, nor of qualifying them to hold office, nor to intermarry
5 with white people; and I will say in addition to this that there is a physical difference between the white and black races which I believe will for ever forbid the two races living together on terms of social and political equality. And inasmuch as they cannot so live, while they do remain together there must be the position of
10 superior and inferior, and I as much as any other man, am in favour of having the superior position assigned to the white man.

However, Lincoln added that to assign 'the superior position..to the white race', was not to say 'the negro should be denied everything'. Lincoln thought it 'quite possible for us to get along without making either slaves or wives of negroes'. Accepting that (free) black and white people might find it difficult to live together in peace, his preferred solution was to re-patriate freed slaves in Africa.

By today's standards, Lincoln and Douglas do not seem particularly far apart. This is perhaps not surprising: both men were moderates as far as their parties were concerned and both were fighting for the middle ground. But the two men did differ in one key respect - and that was to do with slavery. In the final debate, Lincoln spelt out that difference.

> 1 The real issue in this controversy ... is the sentiment on the part of
> one class that looks upon the institution of slavery as a wrong, and
> another class that does not look upon it as wrong ... The
> Republican party ... look upon it as being a moral, social and
> 5 political wrong ... and one of the methods of treating it as a wrong
> is to make provision that it shall grow no larger.

In Lincoln's view the issue was a moral one. Douglas may have regarded the restriction of slavery as desirable but he never once said in public that slavery was a moral evil. Lincoln may not have believed in racial equality but he did believe that blacks and whites shared a common humanity. 'If slavery is not wrong, then nothing is wrong', he said. 'I cannot remember when I did not so think and feel'. He did not expect slavery to wither and die immediately. He did not suppose that 'the ultimate extinction would occur in less than a hundred years at the least' but he was convinced that 'ultimate extinction' should be the goal.

During the debates, Lincoln constantly raised the spectre of the Slave Power conspiracy. Here, he knew, he was on stronger ground. He infuriated Douglas, particularly by claiming that the Supreme Court intended to make slavery legitimate in all the states. However, improbable this may now seem to have been, there is no doubt that Lincoln, like many Northerners, believed it to be a real possibility.

The Illinois result was close. The Republicans received some 125,000 popular votes to the 121,000 for Douglas's Democrats. But Douglas's supporters kept control of the Illinois legislature and the legislature, by 54 votes to 46, re-elected Douglas as Senator. This was a significant triumph for Douglas: he had seen off both the Republican and the Buchanan threat and solidified his leadership of the Northern Democrats. He would, thus, be in a strong position to battle for the Democrat presidential candidacy in 1860.

But not all was good news in the Douglas camp. During the debates with Lincoln, Douglas had said much that alienated Southerners - not least his stressing of the so-called Freeport Doctrine - that voters of a territory could effectively exclude slavery simply by refusing to enact laws that gave legal protection to slave property thus effectively invalidating the Dred Scott ruling. In consequence, his presidential ambitions were unlikely to get much support from the South. The hatred which Buchanan and Southern Democrats felt for Douglas was shown in December 1858 when he was removed from his chairmanship of the Senate Committee on Territories, a position which he had held for ten years.

Lincoln was disappointed by the 1858 result. He had anticipated winning. However, from his personal point of view, everything was far from lost. He had emerged from the Illinois election as a Republican spokesman of national stature, battling Douglas on even terms and clarifying the issues dividing Republicans from Northern Democrats. In 1859-60 Lincoln received a large number of invitations to speak outside Illinois and, as he moved about the North-west addressing enthusiastic audiences, he further enhanced his reputation.

Overall, the 1858 mid-term elections were a disaster for the Northern Democrats. Their representation in the House fell from 53 to 32 (12 of whom were Douglas supporters) with the result that the Republicans now controlled the House. The Republican gains were particularly significant in the crucial lower Northern states. The Republican share of the vote in Pennsylvania, Indiana, Illinois and New Jersey rose from 35 per cent in 1856 to 52 per cent in 1858. The Republicans were helped by the economic depression and by the fact that the American party had effectively disappeared in most Northern states. If the 1858 voting pattern was repeated in 1860 the Republicans would win the presidency. Southerners were well aware of this prospect - and were naturally alarmed. Southern fear was heightened by the actions of John Brown.

7 John Brown's Raid

John Brown had first risen to fame - or infamy - in Kansas. His butchery of five pro-slavers at Pottawotomie had been reported differently in the North and South. Southerners, who had been told a more correct version of events, regarded Brown as a monster and put a price on his head. Northerners, on the other hand, still regarded Brown as a hero - a man who had fought on behalf of slaves. Brown, himself, was still determined to do something decisive for the anti-slavery cause. Now in his late fifties, he saw himself as God's instrument to wipe out slavery - and slaveowners. Some thought he was a madmen. There was certainly a history of insanity in his family. His mother and grandmother had both died insane. Three of his mother's sisters and two of her brothers were intermittently insane. One of his brothers, one of his sisters and one of his sons were also insane.

But many abolitionists believed that Brown was a man of integrity and moral conviction. The fact that he was able to win financial support from hard-headed Northern businessmen is testimony to both his charismatic personality and the intensity of abolitionist sentiment. Shuttling to and fro between Kansas, New England and Canada, Brown plotted some kind of military-style operation against slavery. At first he intended to strike in Kansas. Then in the summer of 1859 he turned his attention to Virginia. Hiring a farm in a remote area near the Maryland-Virginia border, Brown determined to launch a major raid on the Federal arsenal at Harper's Ferry. The aim was to seize the weapons, retreat to the Appalachian mountains and from there spark a great slave revolt. Brown naively assumed that once the crusade began, slaves throughout the South would flock to join him. Unfortunately, it was impossible to inform the slaves in advance of his intentions. This was a major - but by no means the only - flaw in Brown's plan. The fact that there were few slaves in the Harper's Ferry area was another.

In retrospect what is remarkable is that the raid on Harper's Ferry was kept secret. Brown's main financial backers - the 'Secret Six' - although not certain of his precise goal, were aware of his broad intentions. Several influential people were also in the know, including the black abolitionist leader Frederick Douglass who declined to join Brown, convinced that his mission was suicidal. Politicians like William Seward and Floyd, the Secretary of War, who had heard rumours of Brown's intentions, refused to take them seriously.

On the night of 16 October 1859 Brown, five blacks and thirteen whites (including three of his sons) left their Maryland hideout and rode to Harper's Ferry. They captured the arsenal with remarkable ease and also took a number of hostages, including a great grand-nephew of George Washington. A few bewildered slaves were induced or compelled to join Brown's raid. But then things began to go wrong. A train pulled into Harper's Ferry - shots were fired by one of Brown's men - and the first man to die was a free black baggage master working for the railway. Eventually Brown allowed the train to proceed through Harper's Ferry to spread the alarm. Rather than escape to the hills, Brown decided to remain in the arsenal. This was totally irrational. He had no supplies for a siege. Moreover he could hardly spark a great slave revolt holed up in Harper's Ferry.

Brown's position soon became desperate. Excited Harper's Ferry citizens began sniping at Brown's men and Virginia and Maryland state militia units quickly converged on the town, blocking all escape routes. Most of Brown's force eventually took refuge in the fire-engine house at the arsenal. Buchanan sent a detachment of marines, led by Lieutenant Colonel Robert E. Lee, to deal with the situation. A 36 hour siege followed with Brown threatening to kill the hostages and Lee attempting to persuade Brown to give himself up. On 18 October Lee ordered the fire-engine house to be stormed. In the ensuing struggle Brown was wounded and captured along with six of his men. Ten of his 'army' were killed (including two of his sons). Seven other people also lost their lives.

Brown was immediately tried for treason. Refusing a plea of insanity, he determined to die a martyr's death - by so doing helping the anti-slavery cause rather more than his ill-conceived raid had done. At his trial he showed both courage and dignity, even winning the respect of some Southerners. He was quickly found guilty and sentenced to death. On 2 December 1859 he rode to his execution on his own coffin. He said nothing on the scaffold. But in his last letter he wrote: 'I, John Brown am now quite certain that the crimes of this guilty land will never be purged away but with Blood'.

Brown's raid was a crucial event. Coming on the eve of the 1860 presidential election, it raised sectional tensions to new heights. Most

Southerners were appalled at what had happened. Their worst fears had been realised. A Northern abolitionist had tried to stir up a major slave revolt. Southerner's suspected that this was the tip of the iceberg. Aware (from captured correspondence) that Brown had considerable financial support, they suspected that most Northerners sympathised with Brown's action. Some Northerners certainly did see Brown as a noble martyr. Church bells were rung in many Northern towns and villages on the day of his execution. But by no means all Northerners approved the Harper's Ferry raid. Northern Democrats condemned Brown's action out of hand: Douglas announced that the raid on Harper's Ferry had been a 'natural' and 'logical' consequence of the teaching and doctrines of the Republicans. The official Republican line was to dissociate itself from Brown's raid, depicting it as the work of a solitary fanatic. It was, in the eyes of some of its leaders (including Lincoln and Seward), 'fatally wrong' and 'utterly repugnant'.

Few Southerners were reassured by the Republican repudiation of Brown. Most saw the Republicans and abolitionists (like Brown) as inseparable components of an unholy alliance against slavery. 'The Harper's Ferry invasion has advanced the cause of disunion more than any other event that has happened since the formation of its government', said the *Enquirer,* a Richmond newspaper in October 1859. More Southerners now listened to Southern 'fire-eaters', who had long been predicting that something like this was set to happen.

8 The Situation in 1859-60

Over the winter of 1859-60 there were rumours of slave insurrection, prompted by an abolitionist conspiracy, in many Southern states. Local vigilante committees were set up and slave patrols strengthened. Southern state governments purchased additional weapons and Southern militia units drilled rather more than previously.

The first session of the 36th Congress met in December 1859. Both Houses immediately divided along sectional lines. In the House there was a two month contest for the speakership and effective deadlock. Northern and Southern politicians exchanged insults and some members of Congress came armed. 'The only persons who did not have a revolver and knife', commented one Senator, 'are those who have two revolvers.' Southerners opposed all Republican economic measures - free homesteads, higher tariffs and the construction of a Pacific railroad. They claimed, with some justification, that such policies favoured the North at the expense of the South. Buchanan's hopes of purchasing Cuba from Spain failed because Republicans in Congress were not prepared to provide the funds needed. Senator Jefferson Davis's efforts to pass measures that would have established a Federal Slave Code in the territories (and thus stopped territorial legislatures barring slavery by refusing to pass laws protecting the institution) also bit the dust.

By 1860 both Northerners and Southerners carried inflammatory rhetoric to new heights of passion. Northerners feared a conspiracy by the Slave Power. Southerners feared the growing strength of the 'Black Republicans'. Buchanan, who had sought to avoid controversy, had presided over one of the most controversial administrations in American history. Undoubtedly some of his problems arose less from his own actions than from the fact that the forces driving the nation apart were starting to spin out of control by the end of the 1850s. Nevertheless Buchanan's policies, particularly with regard to Kansas, had helped exacerbate the sectional rift. His presidency, in consequence, must be regarded as one of the great failures of leadership in American history.

Making notes on *'The Presidency of James Buchanan'*

This chapter is designed to show what problems Buchanan's administration faced and how it attempted to tackle them. The headings and sub-headings used in the chapter should help you to organise the material and compile a detailed summary of the main events of 1857-60. As you make your notes, try to make your own judgement about the success or failure of Buchanan's policies. It is often interesting to question perceived wisdom and to debunk 'heroes' or, conversely, to defend the reputation of people generally regarded as fools or villains. As is obvious from this chapter, I would find it hard to defend Buchanan. But that should not stop you having a go! Make a list of the difficulties he faced. How many of these were of his own-making? Was he simply unlucky? Should he be pitied rather than blamed?

Source-based questions on *'The Presidency of James Buchanan'*

1 'A House Divided'
Examine the extract from Lincoln's 'House Divided' speech in June 1858 on page 105. Answer the following questions:
a) How might Douglas have responded to Lincoln's charge that this 'government cannot endure permanently half slave and half free'? (5 marks)
b) What evidence does Lincoln use to suggest that there was a Slave Power conspiracy at work? (3 marks)
c) What, in Lincoln's view, were the 'chief bosses' planning to do next? (2 marks)
d) To what extent - if any - was Lincoln suggesting that Civil War was inevitable? (5 marks)

2 The Lincoln-Douglas Debates
Examine the extracts on pages 106-8. Answer the following questions:
a) Summarise Douglas's main arguments in the extract from his first speech. (6 marks)

b) How might Lincoln have answered Douglas's jibe: 'I do not question Mr Lincoln's conscientious belief that the negro was made his equal, and hence is his brother'? (4 marks)
c) To what extent were Douglas's main arguments consistent? (5 marks)
d) To what extent were Lincoln's main arguments consistent? (5 marks)

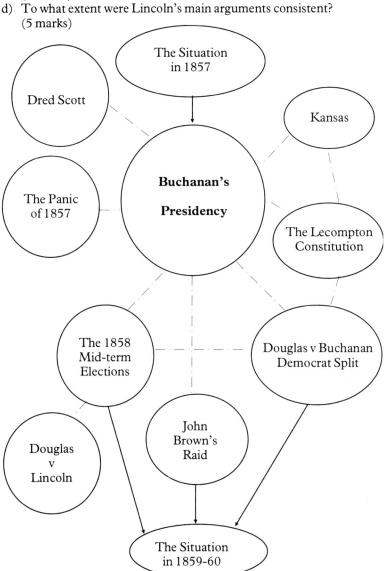

Summary - The Presidency of James Buchanan

CHAPTER 7

The 1860 Election and Secession

1 Introduction

The events of the 1850s had brought a growing number of Southerners to the conclusion that the North had deserted the true principles of the Union. In Southern eyes, it was the North, not the South that had grown 'peculiar'. It was the North that had urbanised, industrialised and absorbed large numbers of immigrants while the South had remained agricultural, Anglo-Saxon and loyal to its roots. Southern 'fire-eaters' claimed that the South would be far better off seceding from the Union and going its own way. Nevertheless, in early 1860 the 'fire-eaters' were far from representative of Southern public opinion. Most Southerners, while united in defence of slavery, still wanted to remain within the Union. However, the prospect of a Republican triumph in 1860 filled many with outrage and dread. A Republican victory might threaten slavery and sow the seeds of more slave uprisings. Submission to the Republicans, declared Southern Democrat Senator Jefferson Davis, 'would be intolerable to a proud people'. If a Republican did become President, then plenty of Southerners were prepared to consider the possibility of secession. The stakes in the November 1860 presidential election, therefore, were alarmingly high.

2 The 1860 Presidential Candidates

If the Republicans were to be defeated in 1860 it seemed essential that the rifts within the Democrat party should somehow be healed. Douglas, determined to run for President, made some efforts to build bridges to the South throughout 1859 and 1860. Rationally he was the South's best hope in 1860: he was the only Democrat who was likely to carry some Northern states - and to win the election the Democrats had to win some free states. But Douglas's stand against the Lecompton constitution and his support for the 'Freeport Doctrine' alienated him from most Southerners. Once seen as one of the South's most reliable friends, he was now regarded as a traitor.

Events at the Democrat convention, which met in April 1860 at Charleston, South Carolina, showed that the party, never mind the country, was very much a house divided against itself. From Douglas's point of view, Charleston, capital of the most 'fire-eating' of all the Southern states, was an unfortunate choice for the convention. The townspeople, many of whom crowded into the convention hall to witness proceedings, made clear their opposition to Douglas. But Douglas's aspiration to gain the Democrat nomination was far from hopeless. In the convention Northern Democrats outnumbered

Southerners and most Northerners were determined to nominate Douglas. They were aware they faced political extinction at home unless they seized control of the party and ended its pro-Southern policies.

The rifts within the Democrat party could not be healed. When Northern Democrats succeeded in blocking a proposal which would have pledged the party to protect the rights of slaveholders in the territories, some 50 delegates from the lower South walked out of the convention. Unable to reach consensus on policy, the Democrats found it equally impossible to nominate a presidential candidate. Although Douglas had the support of the majority of the delegates, he failed to win the two-thirds majority which Democrat candidates were (traditionally) expected to achieve. After 57 fruitless ballots the Democrat convention agreed to reconvene at Baltimore in June.

Some of the Southern delegates who had left the Charleston convention, attempted to take up their seats at Baltimore. However, the convention, dominated by Douglas supporters, preferred to take a number of hastily elected pro-Douglas delegates from the lower South. This led to another mass Southern walk-out.. With so many Southern delegates gone and a simple majority rule instituted, Douglas easily won the nomination of the 'official' convention. Meanwhile, the Southern delegates set up their own 'rump' convention in another hall in Baltimore and proceeded to nominate the current Vice President John Breckinridge of Kentucky on a platform that called for the Federal government to 'protect the rights of persons and property in the Territories'. Yet another Southern convention, meeting in Richmond, ratified the action of the 'rump' convention at Baltimore.

Breckinridge reluctantly agreed to run. He did not stand on a secessionist ticket. Indeed he was supported by many old guard Democrats, including Cass, Pierce and Buchanan (the last three titular heads of the Democrat party), by eight of the ten Northern Democrat Senators, and by 80 per cent of the Democrat representatives in the House. Nevertheless, it was clear that the Democrat party had split along sectional lines. Most Northern Democrats supported Douglas. In consequence Breckinridge's chances of victory were nil. Oddly most Southern Democrats were far from despondent at events and both moderates and 'fire-eaters' campaigned enthusiastically for Breckinridge. The fact that Southerners, unable to control the Democrat party, had petulantly 'seceded' from it and put forward their own candidate, was perhaps something of a dress rehearsal - an indication of the South's likely action in November 1860 should the Republicans triumph.

The Democrat split is often seen as a major explanation of the 1860 Republican success and thus a major cause of the Civil War. However, even without the Democrat schism, the Republican party - which simply had to carry the North - was favourite to win. The Democrat split may actually have weakened, the Republicans, if only because Douglas was now able to campaign in the North without the embarrassment of having to try to maintain a united national Democrat party. It could be that Northerners would be more likely to vote for him, given that he had effectively cut his links with the South.

The Republican convention met in May 1860 at Chicago in the 'Wigwam' - a huge wooden building which could accommodate over 10,000 people. Virtually all the 466 delegates represented Northern constituencies. The delegates found it easier to agree on a platform than a presidential candidate. In 1856 the Republicans had been largely a single-issue, free-soil party. To win in 1860 the party needed to broaden its appeal in the North. Republican leaders had concluded they needed to forge an economic programme to complement their advocacy of free soil. The 1860 Republican platform, therefore, called for higher protective tariffs (popular in Pennsylvania), free 160 acre homesteads for settlers heading west (popular in the Midwestern states) and government support for a northern Pacific railway. The Republicans were still opposed to any extension of slavery: popular sovereignty was castigated as being a 'deception and fraud'. If anything, however, the platform was a shade more moderate than the 1856 platform. It specifically promised that the party had no intention of interfering with slavery where it already existed; it did not brand slavery as a 'relic of barbarism' (as it had done in 1856); and it condemned John Brown's raid on Harper's Ferry as 'the gravest of crimes'. The Republican delegates were prepared to do a certain amount of trimming in order to appeal to as many shades of opinion as possible and so capture the battleground states - Pennsylvania, Indiana, Illinois and New Jersey.

William Seward was the favourite to win the Republican presidential nomination. Governor of New York for four years and a Senator for 12 years, he was the best known Republican politician. But the fact that he had been a major figure in public life for so long meant, inevitably, that he had many enemies, even (perhaps especially!) in New York. Although he was actually a pragmatic, calculating politician who disdained extremism, he was seen - wrongly - as holding radical views on slavery. Moreover, he had a long record of hostility to nativism. His nomination, therefore, might make potential voters, especially ex-Know Nothings, think twice about voting Republican. A stop-Seward movement gathered momentum across the North in the weeks before the Republican convention.

There were a number of other potential Republican candidates. These included Edward Bates of Missouri, an ex-Know Nothing who was conservative and not obviously Republican. Salmon Chase, the Senator and ex-governor of Ohio, had some support but was regarded as too radical on the slavery issue. Simon Cameron, who came from the crucial state of Pennsylvania, was another contender: he was a typical political 'boss' with an unsavoury reputation for corruption. The main opponent of Seward turned out to be Abraham Lincoln. Lincoln had several things in his favour. He came from the key state of Illinois and had gained a national reputation as a result of his debates with Douglas in 1858. While denying he held any presidential ambitions, in 1859-60 he had travelled over 4,000 miles and made dozens of speeches throughout the North, gaining friends and making himself known. Respected for his solid opposition to slavery expansion, he was nevertheless seen as being a moderate. The fact that it was difficult to attach an ideological label to him meant that he was able to appear to be all things to all men. He had relatively few enemies. He had opposed the Know Nothings but not conspicuously. He was opposed to the prohibition of alcohol - but was himself teetotal. The fact that he had little or no administrative experience helped his reputation for honesty and integrity. His career seemed to symbolise the self-help, 'rags to riches' American dream: he was portrayed as the common man made good. By May 1860 Lincoln was almost everyone's second favourite candidate.

Lincoln's presidential ambitions were helped by the convention being held at Chicago (in Illinois), chosen at a suggestion of one of Lincoln's friend's who had argued that it was a good neutral site given that Illinois had no presidential candidate! As a result Lincoln's campaign managers had no difficulty packing the Wigwam with Lincoln supporters, many with counterfeit tickets, who made considerable noise in his favour. Lincoln (who did not attend the convention) was also fortunate in having a skillful campaign 'team' working for him on the floor of the convention.

Seward's best hope was to win on the first ballot. He won 173 and a half votes: a majority - but not the 233 votes (half the 466 delegates present) needed for an absolute majority. Lincoln won 102 votes on the first ballot: well-behind Seward but more than twice the votes of any of the other contenders. With the race now clearly between Seward and Lincoln, other candidates began to drop out. Most of their votes drifted to Lincoln. The second ballot was very close. By the third ballot there was an irresistible momentum in Lincoln's favour, helped in part by the sheer noise in the convention hall.

Murat Halstead, editor of the *Cincinnati Commercial,* and one of the most famous journalists of the day, vividly described the excitement.

1 The deed was done. There was a moment's silence. The nerves of
the thousands, which through the hours of suspense had been
subjected to terrible tension, relaxed, and as deep breaths of relief
were taken, there was a noise in the Wigwam like the rush of a great
5 wind in the van of a storm - and in another breath, the storm was
there. There were thousands cheering with the energy of insanity
...
    The city was wild with delight. The 'Old Abe' men formed
processions and bore rails through the streets. Torrents of liquor
10 were poured down the throats of the multitude ... I left the city on

the night train ... every seat full and people standing in the aisles
and corners. I never before saw a company of persons so prostrated
by continued excitement. The Lincoln men were not able to
respond to the cheers which went up along the [rail]road for 'Old
15 Abe'. They had not only done their duty in that respect, but
exhausted their capacity. At every station where there was a village
... there were tar barrels burning, drums beating, boys carrying
rails, and guns, great and small, banging away.

Another party was also to mount a challenge for the presidency in 1860.
This was the Constitutional Unionist party. Composed mainly of
ex-Southern Whigs and American party supporters, its main strength lay
in the upper South where American party candidates had continued to
do well in the late 1850s. The Constitutional Unionists held their first
national convention in Baltimore in May 1860, nominating John Bell of
Tennessee, a large slaveholder, as their presidential candidate. The
party had the shortest platform in American political history: 'The
Constitution of the Country, the Union of the States and the
Enforcement of the Laws of the United States'. Essentially the
Constitutional Unionists wanted to remove the slavery question from
the political arena, thus relieving sectional strife. Denouncing the
Republicans as abolitionist fanatics and Breckinridge's Democrats as
disunionists, the Constitutional Unionists' aim was to weaken Lincoln's
support in the lower North, so denying him a majority in the electoral
college. The election of President would then have to be decided in the
House of Representatives where anything could happen.

3 The Election Campaign and Results

The election campaign was largely sectional. In the North the main fight
was between Lincoln and Douglas. Bell and Breckinridge fought it out
in the South. (Lincoln was not even on the ballot in ten Southern states.)
Douglas was the only candidate who actively involved himself in the
campaign. The other three opted for the traditional 'mute tribune' role.
Throughout the campaign, Lincoln remained at home in Springfield,
Illinois. He received visitors, answered correspondence and conferred
with Republican party chiefs: but otherwise he said nothing. His
response to those who pleaded with him to break his silence was 'read
my speeches'. Some historians have criticised Lincoln, claiming he
might have made some efforts to reassure Southerners that he was not a
'Black Republican' or a threat to their section. But Lincoln (like the
leaders of his party) believed that it was best to say nothing. After all, he
could hardly go out of his way to appease the South: this would have
done his cause no good in the North - and retaining strong Northern
support seemed more important than worrying about Southern threats.
Like most Republicans in 1860, Lincoln perhaps did not take the

Southern threat of secession as seriously as he should have. Perhaps this was a 'cardinal error'. But even now it is difficult to see what Lincoln could have done - or said - to allay Southern anxiety, given that the very existence of the Republican party was offensive to the South.

Although Lincoln, Bell and Breckinridge did not personally campaign, this did not prevent their supporters campaigning for them. The Republican party, in particular, had a good organisation and plenty of money: in consequence, the North was flooded with campaign literature. Republican supporters (still known as 'Wide Awakes') held torchlight processions and carried wooden rails. These embodied the notion that Lincoln was the common man who had once split wood for rails. (Ironically Lincoln hated rural life and had worked hard to escape from it!) Republican propaganda, inevitably, concentrated on the Slave Power conspiracy. Southern Democrats, on the other hand, stereotyped all Northerners as 'Black Republicans' set on abolishing slavery. Lincoln, depicted as either a chimpanzee or a bloodthirsty tyrant, was often burned in effigy. But, a few 'fire-eaters' apart, most of Breckinridge's supporters did not draw attention to the fact that they might become disunionists if Lincoln triumphed.

The October 1860 state election results in Pennsylvania and Indiana indicated a Republican victory in November. Douglas read the signs clearly: 'Mr Lincoln is the next President. We must try to save the Union. I will go South'. Suffering from ill-health and at some personal risk, Douglas campaigned in the South. His theme was much the same wherever he spoke: 'If Lincoln is elected', he told an audience in Montgomery, Alabama, 'he must be inaugurated'. Accusing Southern disunionists of desiring Lincoln's election so that it might be used as an excuse for secession, he warned Southerners of the dangerous consequences of secession. His words fell largely on deaf ears. Perhaps the best hope for the three anti-Republican parties was to agree to end their differences and unite against Lincoln in the battleground Northern states. In some states efforts at 'fusion' were made but these efforts were too little and too late and were bedevilled by the bitterness that existed between Breckinridge's, Douglas's and Bell's supporters.

In November 1860 81 per cent of the American electorate voted. Bell won 593,000 votes carrying the upper South states of Virginia, Kentucky, and Tennessee. Although he won 39 per cent of the Southern vote, he won only 5 per cent of the free states vote and took no state out of the Lincoln column. Breckinridge won 843,000 popular votes: 45 per cent of the Southern vote but only 5 per cent of the free states' vote. He won 11 of the 15 slave states and thus won 72 electoral college votes. Douglas won a respectable 1,383,000 popular votes. His support came mainly from the North where he won the vote of most Irish and German Catholics and other traditional Democrat voters, especially in the Mid-west. But he obtained only 12 per cent of the Southern popular vote and won only two states, Missouri and half New Jersey. He thus came a dismal last in terms of electoral college votes. Lincoln won 1,866,000 popular votes - 40 per cent of the total vote and 10 per cent more than Douglas, his nearest challenger. Although he got no votes at all in ten Southern states, he won 54 per cent of the Northern vote and, except for New Jersey, carried all the 18 free states. He thus won a comfortable majority (180 to 123) in the electoral college and became the new President.

Interestingly the South had not proved to be 'solid'. Breckinridge won under 50 per cent of the vote in the slave states as a whole. Not that this made any real difference. Lincoln would have won the election if the South had voted solidly for Breckinridge. Lincoln had won only 40 per cent of the vote but all his votes were strategically positioned in the North. It was in the North where Lincoln had to be challenged. Douglas came close in Illinois, Indiana and California: if Douglas had carried these states Lincoln would not have won the election.

Would Northerners have voted for Lincoln if they had known that his election meant secession and Civil War? Who knows? Like Lincoln, most Northerners believed that those Southerners who talked of secession were bluffing and that the time had come to call their bluff. Most Northerners voted for Lincoln because he seemed to represent their section. A vote for Lincoln was a vote against the Democrats and against the Slave Power. Few Northerners had much notion of what the Slave Power actually was, but most were convinced it existed and posed a threat to the North. Most Northerners, while not wishing to get rid of slavery immediately, considered it a moral evil and had no wish to see it expand. If it could no longer expand, there was every chance it would ultimately wither and die. Slavery and the Slave Power, however, were not the only concern of Northerners. They voted Republican for other reasons. Nativism had not disappeared with the demise of the Know Nothings. Many Northerners were still anti-Catholic and anti-immigrant. Although the Republicans took an ambiguous stand on nativist issues, anti-Catholic Northerners had little option but to vote Republican, if only because the Democrat party remained the home of the Irish and German Catholics. Many Northerners were also impressed by the proposed Republican economic measures.

The corruption issue was also of some importance. In June 1860 a House investigative committee had found corruption at every level of Buchanan's government. The corruption charges, well publicised by the Republicans, had tarnished the Democrat party as a whole: Republicans had been able to brand the Buchanan administration as 'the Buchaneers'. Lincoln - 'honest Abe' - had a reputation for integrity. Even Douglas admitted that he was 'one of the most frank, honest men in political life'. Senator Grimes of Iowa went as far as to state that, 'Our triumph was achieved more because of Lincoln's honesty and the known corruption of the Democrats than because of the negro question'. This is probably to over state the case. But it is certainly a useful reminder that the 1860 election was not just to do with slavery.

4 Secession

Lincoln's victory was to be the green light that the secessionists had been waiting for. This need not have been so. Rationally, there were excellent reasons why the Southern states should not secede from the Union. Lincoln's election posed no immediate threat to the 'peculiar institution'. He had promised he would not interfere directly with slavery in those states where it existed. Even had he harboured secret ambitions to do away with slavery, there was little he could actually do. Presidential power was strictly limited by the Constitution. Lincoln would have needed massive support from Congress before he could have taken any sweeping action. There was no way he would get such support. The Democrat party, divided though it was, still controlled both Houses of Congress. Southerners still dominated the Supreme Court. The fate of all the presidential administrations of the 1850s suggested that control of the executive branch was likely to weaken the party in power rather than strengthen it. It was unlikely that the Republicans - a new and heterogeneous coalition - would be able to unite behind many concrete proposals for very long. There were other considerations. If the Southern states left the Union this would mean abandoning an enforceable Fugitive Slave Act: slaves would easily be able to flee to the North. Nor would secession necessarily prevent further John Brown-type raids on the South. Finally, and perhaps most important of all, secession could well lead to civil war which might do far more to threaten the institution of slavery than Lincoln's election.

However, many Southerners did not regard things so calmly. Southern political power had shrunk to the point where a Northern anti-slavery party, with no pretence of support in the South, could capture the presidency. As far as most Southerners were concerned Lincoln was an unknown quantity. Given that few of them had ever seen any of his supporters, much less the man himself, they were inclined to believe the worst: he was depicted as a rabid abolitionist who would encourage slave insurrections. As President, he would be in a position to appoint judges, customs collectors and postmasters in the South. Such appointments might provide the nucleus of a Southern Republican party - a long-term threat to slavery. In the meantime Republicans would be in a position to move against slavery in Washington DC. They might well be able to weaken or repeal the Fugitive Slave Act. They could, over time, win control of the Supreme Court. Above all, the Republican stand against the expansion of slavery threatened to strike at the vital interests of the South. Southerners feared they would be encircled by a swelling majority of free states and that, ultimately, slavery would be voted out of existence.

Regardless of party affiliation or political beliefs, Southerners felt tremendously wronged. For more than a generation they had seen themselves as the aggrieved innocents in an unequal sectional struggle that unleashed more and more Northern aggressions on Southern rights. They believed they had been denied their fair share of the Federal territories and unfairly taxed through high tariffs to subsidise Northern industry. Most felt their honour - a powerful force at every level of Southern society - was at stake. Honour and self-respect demanded that a stand be taken against the latest Northern outrage, the election of a Republican President. Throughout the South there was a strange mixture of moods - hysteria, indignation, despondency and elation. There were rumours of slave uprisings, following visits by mysterious Yankee strangers, and reports of slaves burning down property and poisoning wells and murdering their owners. (All the rumours turned out to be false.) 'Fire-eaters' like William Yancey of Alabama and Barnwell Rhett of South Carolina who had agitated for years for the cause of Southern independence, were able to capitalise on the mood. Long on the fringe of Southern politics, they now found themselves supported by many 'mainstream' politicians.

But secession was not inevitable. There was still much Unionist sympathy in the South. (Anti-Breckinridge candidates in the 1860 elections, after all, had won 49 per cent of the vote even in the seven lower South states.) Nor was there any great Southern organisation that might organise a secessionist movement. Most Southerners were loyal to their state rather than to the notion of the 'South'. There had never been a Southern nation. Most fire-eaters knew that the notion of a 'solid' South was a myth. Virtually every state was rife with tensions, often between the yeoman-dominated backcountry and the planter-dominated lowcountry. There was not even unity on the best political strategy to now adopt. Many Southerners believed that Lincoln's election was ground enough for secession. But others thought it was best to wait until Lincoln committed an overt hostile act against the South. Those who favoured immediate secession also faced a major dilemma: if they forced the issue, they might destroy the Southern unity that they were seeking to create. But if they waited for unity, they might never act. How to force the issue was another problem. If individual states acted alone, there was the danger that they would receive no support from other Southern states. This had been the problem South Carolina had faced in the nullification crisis of 1832. Yet attempting to organise a mass Southern move for secession, might ensure nothing happened - as had been the case in the crisis of 1849-50.

However, events now moved with a rapidity which few had foreseen. On November 10 South Carolina's state legislature, which had remained in session because of the likelihood of a crisis, called for elections to a special state convention to meet on 17 December 1860. This convention would decide whether the state would or would not secede. The speed of South Carolina's action was vital. It accelerated the tempo and sparked off a chain reaction elsewhere. Alabama, Mississippi, Georgia, Louisiana and Florida all began similar convention procedures. In Texas governor Sam Houston, who opposed disunion, was able to delay proceedings but only by a few weeks.

Individual states committed themselves - in the first instance - to individual action. However, it was also clear that Southerners were equally committed to joint action. There was liaison between the Southern states at various levels but particularly between Southern Congressmen who met frequently in caucus. When Congress met in early December, 7 Senators and 23 representatives from 9 Southern states issued a public address: 'The argument is exhausted ... We are satisfied the honour, safety and independence of the Southern people are to be found only in a Southern Confederacy - a result to be obtained only by separate state secession'. Separate state secession was not long in coming. On 20 December 1860 the South Carolina convention voted 169-0 for secession. Four days later the state defended its action in a 'Declaration of Causes of Secession'.

1 And now the State of South Carolina having resumed her separate and equal place among nations, deems it due to herself, to the remaining United States of America, and to the nations of the world, that she should declare the immediate causes which have
5 led to this act ... We affirm that these ends for which this Government was instituted have been defeated, and the Government itself has been destructive of them by the action of the nonslaveholding States. Those States have assumed the right of deciding upon the propriety of our domestic institutions; and have
10 denied the rights of property established in fifteen of the States and recognized by the Constitution; they have denounced as sinful the institution of Slavery ... They have encouraged and assisted thousands of our slaves to leave their homes; and those who remain, have been incited by emissaries, books, and pictures, to
15 servile insurrection. For twenty-five years this agitation has been steadily increasing, until it has now secured to its aid the power of the common Government ... A geographical line has been drawn across the Union, and all the States north of that line have united in the election of a man to the high office of President of the United
20 States whose opinions and purposes are hostile to Slavery.

Having justified her decision to secede, South Carolina also appointed commissioners to visit other Southern states to persuade them to secede and to propose a meeting for the creation of a provisional government for those states which did secede. This convention was to meet in Montgomery, Alabama on 4 February 1861. In late December 1860 and early January 1861 the election of delegates for conventions that would decide whether states seceded or remained in the Union took place in the six other lower South states in an atmosphere of great excitement and tension.

The convention elections cause difficulties for historians. Southern voters generally had a choice between 'immediate secessionists' and 'cooperationists'. Although the stand point of the immediate secessionists was clear, the same cannot be said for the cooperationists who represented a wide spectrum of opinion. Some were genuine secessionists but believed the time was not yet right: others were essentially unionists, opposed to the notion of secession. It is difficult for historians today to determine the exact distribution of voters along this spectrum. Were voters who voted for cooperationists showing their opposition to secession or simply showing their opposition to secession now? The situation is even more confused because some candidates committed themselves to no position: they ran as influential local leaders who would make up their minds as events developed. Many were returned unopposed. In consequence, it is hard to gauge the real state of Southern public opinion from the results.

In Mississippi, 12,218 voted for cooperationist candidates. 16,800 voted for immediate secession. On 9 January 1861 the Mississippi convention voted by 85 votes to 15 for secession. The following day the Florida convention voted 62 to 7 for secession. (Cooperationists in Florida won over 35 per cent of the vote.) In Alabama the secessionists won 35,600 votes, the cooperationists 28,100 votes. On 11 January Alabama voted to secede by 61 votes to 39. The voting in Georgia was even closer. Secessionist candidates won 44,152 votes, cooperationists 41,632. The Georgia convention voted to secede on 19 January by 208 votes to 89. In Louisiana the voting was also close: secessionists won 20,214 votes, the cooperationists 18,451. On 26 January the Louisiana convention voted to secede by 113 votes to 17. The situation in Texas was complicated because of the delaying tactics introduced by Unionist Governor Sam Houston. He refused to convene the Texas legislature. But an influential group of secessionist leaders called for the election of delegates to a convention and on 1 February that convention voted for secession by 166 votes to 8. Unlike the other states, Texas then had a referendum to ratify the convention's action. Secession was eventually approved by 44,317 votes to 13,020.

5 A Slave Power Conspiracy?

Republicans in the North, including Lincoln, saw the events in the South as a continuation of the Slave Power conspiracy. They claimed that a small number of secessionist planters had guided an excited electorate into secession. Most Southerners were not, they claimed, really committed to secession. The debate about whether secession was led by a small aristocratic clique or was a genuinely democratic act has continued. Certainly slaveholders dominated politics in many lower

South states and large planters often had considerable influence. Texas apart, the states did not submit their secession ordinances to the people for ratification. Interestingly as well, fewer people voted in the convention elections than had voted in the November 1860 presidential election. (The short time allotted for campaigning and the uncontested nature of many of the local races probably held down the vote.) The key to the victory of the secessionists was their strength in the plantation districts. Areas with few slaves tended to vote strongly against disunion. Conversely, secession sentiment was strongest wherever the percentage of slaves was highest. In the view of David Potter, 'To a much greater degree than the slaveholders desired, secession had become a slaveowners' movement'. Potter was of the opinion that a secessionist minority, with a clear purpose, seized the momentum and at a time of passion and confusion, was able to win mass support.

However, Potter conceded that the secessionists acted in an 'open and straightforward' manner. In most respects the South was as democratic as the North. By no means all the secessionists were great planters. (And by no means all the great planters supported secession: some led the fight to remain in the Union.) There seems little doubt that there was considerable support for secession throughout the lower South, even among non-slave-holders. While it is true that secessionists opposed efforts by cooperationists to submit the secession ordinances to a popular referendum, another election to ratify secession would probably have been superfluous. The Southern electorate had made its position clear in the convention elections. There was thus no conspiracy to thwart the expressed will of the majority in any state. Moreover, many of those who had not voted for immediate secession were quite prepared to support it. Almost all Southerners believed that secession was a theoretical right. Faced with a vengeful North, most were convinced the South had every right to secede to protect its interests, in particular its property and liberties. Most, while hoping they would not have to fight, were prepared to do so if necessary. Throughout the lower South, white males rushed to join military companies which pledged to defend Southern independence.

Making notes on *'The 1860 Election and Secession'*

Your notes on this chapter should give you an understanding of the main candidates in the 1860 presidential election, the main issues at stake, and the main reasons why Lincoln triumphed. They should also help you understand the process by which the seven states of the lower South came to secede. As you read the chapter try to identify why Northerners voted for Lincoln and why Southerners regarded Lincoln's election triumph as a reason to break up the Union. You should have opinions, supported by evidence, about whether Northerners and Southerners were wise or foolish to vote - and act - as they did. It is also worth deciding whether you think the Southern states had the right to leave the Union. In 1860-1 few people in Britain had much sympathy with the South's stand on slavery. But many felt the South had every right to secede, if her people so wished.

Source-based questions on 'The 1860 Election and Secession'

1 Lincoln's nomination

Read Halstead's account on page 117. Answer the following questions:
a) Why did Lincoln's supporters carry rails? (2 marks)
b) Comment on Halstead's observation: 'They [the Lincoln men] had not only done their duty in that respect [cheering] but exhausted their capacity.' (3 marks)
c) How good a source is Halstead for providing an understanding of what occurred at the Republican convention? (5 marks)

2 South Carolina's 'Declaration of Causes of Secession'

Read the extract on page 123. Answer the following questions:
a) Comment on the statement that South Carolina had now 'resumed her separate and equal place among nations'. (3 marks)
b) What are the main reasons used by South Carolina to defend its action? (5 marks)
c) How might a pro-Republican newspaper have responded to South Carolina's 'Declaration'? (7 marks)

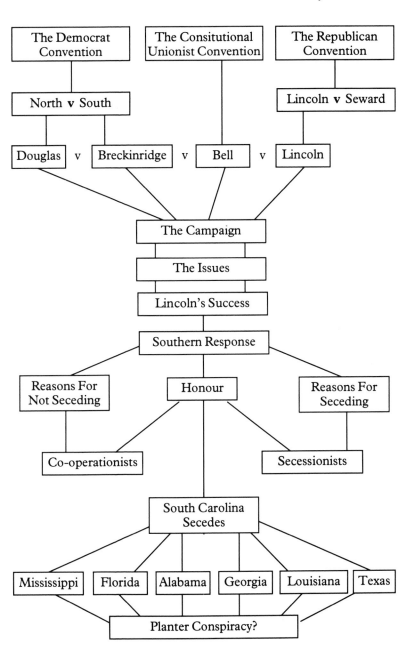

Summary - The 1860 Election and Secession

CHAPTER 8

The Outbreak of Civil War

1 Introduction

Few Americans expected war in February 1861. Most Northerners believed that the seceded states were bluffing or thought that an extremist minority had seized power against the wishes of the majority. Either way, the seceded states would soon be back in the Union: the Southern bluff would be called; or the Unionist majority would assert itself. In contrast, most Southerners thought that the North would accept the inevitable and not fight to preserve the Union. Many Americans were confident that some kind of compromise deal could be arranged which would bring the seceded states back into the Union. These hopes and expectations were not to be realised. By April 1861 the United States were no longer united: they were at war. Was this the fault of blundering politicians? Or was the rift between North and South so great that war was largely inevitable?

2 The Confederacy

On 4 February 1861 the delegates of the seceded states met at Montgomery, Alabama. The meeting was to launch the Confederate government, write a provisional constitution and choose a provisional president and vice president. Each of the seven seceded states was allowed the same number of delegates as it had previously had Congressmen in Washington. But each state was allowed only one vote. Chosen by the secession conventions, the vast majority of the 50 men who met at Montgomery were either lawyers or planters. 49 were slaveowners. 21 owned at least 20 slaves and one owned 473. Almost all had extensive political experience. 60 per cent had been Democrats: the other 40 per cent were ex-Whigs. All in all they comprised a broad cross section of the South's traditional political leadership. Almost half of the delegates were cooperationists who had been either outright opponents or at best lukewarm supporters of secession. Fire-eating radicals were distinctly under-represented at Montgomery. The convention, desperate to win the support of the eight upper South slave states which had not yet seceded from the Union, did its best to project a moderate image.

The Confederate Constitution - unanimously approved by the Provisional Congress in March and ratified by all seven states in April 1861 - was very closely modelled on the American Constitution. The main differences were features that more closely protected the institution of slavery and guaranteed state rights. Unlike the American Constitution, the Confederate Constitution actually called a slave a slave. While the Constitution placed extra emphasis on respect for state rights, in some respects the new Confederate government had more power than the US government. The President, for example, although limited to a single term, was to remain in office for six years allowing more opportunity to implement policies.

The choice of President engendered the most interest. There was no shortage of potential candidates (especially from Georgia) but from the start there was a strong current in favour of Jefferson Davis of Mississippi and on 9 February the convention unanimously elected him provisional President. Davis seemed a good appointment. Educated at West Point, he had served with distinction in the Mexican War, helping to win the battle of Buena Vista. A successful planter, he had served as Secretary of War and as Democrat Senator for Mississippi. A man of dignity, experience and integrity, he had long been a champion of Southern rights but was by no means a fire-eater. He was thus highly acceptable to both the lower and upper South. Davis, who expected that the North would fight to preserve the Union, would have preferred a military command. Nevertheless, he dutifully accepted the post. Alexander Stephens, from Georgia, was elected vice president. As the foremost anti-secessionist in the South, he seemed the logical choice to attract and weld cooperationists to the new government. To satisfy the geographical balance, Davis's cabinet was made up of men from each state of the Confederacy except from his own state Mississippi.

The Provisional Congress went on to pass a spate of legislation to set the machinery of the new government in motion. It re-enacted all the US laws not inconsistent with the Confederate Constitution. It adopted the Stars and Bars as the national flag. It dispatched commissioners to foreign powers and to Washington to negotiate for Federal property within the Confederacy. It passed major pieces of financial legislation, notably the issue of $15 million worth of Treasury bonds, and also created both a small regular army and a larger provisional army. In little more than a month, the Montgomery delegation had set up a viable government, elected executive officers and begun the formidable task of setting the Confederacy on a war footing.

On 18 February Davis took the oath of office as President. In his inaugural speech he asked only that the Confederacy be left alone. Like most Southerners, he was generally confident about the ability of the Confederacy to survive and prosper. Many Southerners (but not Davis) did not expect the North seriously to oppose the secessionist move. Most expected British economic and political support, had faith in 'King Cotton' and hoped to expand southwards into the Caribbean and Central America. However, Confederate leaders did have some concerns - not least the fact that no states from the upper South had yet agreed to join the Confederacy. The seven original Confederate states comprised only 10 per cent of America's population and had only 5 per cent of its industrial capacity. Support from Virginia, in particular, was vital if the Confederacy was to have much chance of survival.

3 The Upper South

In January 1861 the state legislatures of Arkansas, Virginia, Missouri, Tennessee and North Carolina all called elections for state conventions to decide on secession. But various limits were placed on the conventions' powers. Virginia, for example, gave voters the option of requiring a popular referendum on any action the convention might take. Arkansas and Tennessee empowered their voters to elect delegates to conventions but also to decide whether conventions should be held. The results of the February elections proved that the upper South was far less secessionist-inclined than the lower South. In Virginia the secessionists suffered, in Potter's view, a 'shattering defeat'. Only 32 immediate secessionists won seats in a convention with 152 members. The situation, from a secessionist viewpoint, was even worse elsewhere. Tennessee voted 69,387 to 57,798 against calling a convention; and voted for Unionists rather than secessionists if the proposed convention had met. North Carolinians repeated the Tennessee pattern. Arkansas voted for a convention but most of the elected delegates were Unionists who voted to reject secession. Secessionists made no headway whatsoever in Missouri. Elsewhere in the upper South, the Kentucky legislature refused to call a convention. In Maryland, the Unionist Governor Hicks refused even to call a special session of the state legislature. In Delaware the state legislature voted 'unqualified disapproval' of secession. The result was that by the end of February, secession seemed to have burnt itself out. Developments in the upper South provided some hope for Lincoln and the Republicans.

A number of reasons have been put forward to explain why the upper South states did not vote immediately for secession. Most important was the fact that these states had a much smaller stake in slavery than the lower South. Less than 30 per cent of the upper South population was black.. Many border-state whites could contemplate and even accept the eventual end of slavery. In Maryland nearly half the blacks were already free. Lacking the passionate commitment of the lower South to defending slavery, Unionists were able to mobilise anti-secessionist majorities. Slavery was not the only issue. The upper South had more reason to fear the economic consequences of secession. Most border states had close economic ties with the North. Moreover, if war came the upper South would be the likeliest battleground. In many respects - given that it had voted strongly for Bell and Douglas, not Breckinridge in 1860 - the upper South voting came as no surprise.

But although the upper South states continued to remain within the Union, their support for that Union should not be exaggerated. Many people in the border states had a deep distrust of Lincoln and the Republicans. The legislatures of Virginia and Tennessee made it clear that they would oppose any attempt to force the seceding states back into the Union. If it came to the crunch, there would be many in the upper South who would put their Southern affiliations first.

4 The Search for Compromise

Lincoln did not take over until March 1861. Believing there was little he could do. Unil then, he remained in his own home at Springfield. In the meantime President Buchanan, who was more aware of the dangers of the situation than many Republican leaders, continued officially to hold the reins of power. Buchanan believed that secession was unconstitutional. But he also believed that any action on his part to try to coerce the Confederate states back into the Union was similarly unconstitutional. Aware that he had no popular mandate to rule, his main concern was not to provoke an armed conflict with the seceding states. He took no action, therefore, as Federal institutions throughout the South - forts, arsenals, custom houses and post offices - were taken over by the Confederate states. Some Republican newspapers declared that he ought to be impeached for his inactivity. But Buchanan did make one vital decision. He determined not to recall the Federal garrisons at Fort Sumter (in Charleston harbour) and Fort Pickens (Pensacola, Florida). This was to have major repercussions.

Historians have criticised Buchanan, not so much for his unwillingness to use force against the Confederacy, but more for his failure to do more to seek a compromise solution. A Northerner with strong Southern connections, he would seem to have been in a strong position to have initiated moves which might have brought about a peaceful solution to the crisis. Alan Nevins particularly criticised Buchanan for not calling a national convention immediately after the 1860 election. But in fairness to Buchanan, it is difficult to see what exactly he (or a national convention) could have done. After the presidential election the lower Southern states were set upon leaving the Union. Moreover most Republicans did not trust Buchanan, whom they considered a Southern puppet. Buchanan did call on the Republican party to appease the South but his suggestions that the new government should commit itself to acquiring Cuba or making concessions in the Western territories were rejected out of hand by leading Republicans.

In Buchanan's view Congress had more responsibility for finding a solution to the crisis than himself. The second session of the 36th Congress met in December 1860. Most of the Congressmen from the Confederate states did not attend and those who did soon resigned their seats. However, there were many Congressmen, particularly Northern Democrats and representatives from the upper South, who hoped to work out a compromise. Both the House of Representatives and the Senate quickly established committees to explore plans of conciliation. The House Committee, with 33 members, proved to be too cumbersome. The Senate Committee of 13 was more effective. John Crittenden, a slave-holding Kentucky Unionist with a reputation for fairness, played a significant part in proceedings.

After much deliberation, the Senate Committee recommended a package of compromise proposals (which came out under Crittenden's name). The main idea was to extend the Missouri Compromise line to the Pacific, thus giving the South some hope of slavery expansion. Slavery would be recognised south of 36° 30 in all present territories, as well as those 'hereafter acquired'. The Crittenden proposals also called for an Amendment to the Constitution to guarantee that there would be no interference with slavery in those states where it already existed. As other sops to the South, Congress would be forbidden to abolish slavery in the District of Columbia, would not be allowed to interfere with the inter-state slave trade, and fugitive slave holders would be compensated by the Federal government if they lost their 'property'.

Republicans were not impressed by Crittenden's proposals which seemed to smack more of surrender than compromise. Many still denied the existence of any real crisis: they interpreted events in the South as Southern bluster to force the North to make concessions. They believed the time had come to stand firm. With the withdrawal of the Southern delegates, Republican strength in Congress had increased significantly. The House of Representatives rejected Crittenden's compromise proposals by 113 votes to 80. The voting in the Senate was closer - 25 votes to 23.

Congressional efforts to find a compromise were not the only ones. In February 1861 a Peace Convention met in Washington, at the request of Virginia, to see if it was possible to find measures that would bring the seceded states back into the Union. 133 delegates (including some of the most famous names in American politics) attended and 21 states were represented. But the Convention was boycotted by a few free states and, more significantly, the Confederate states ignored the invitation to attend. After three weeks deliberation, the Convention supported proposals similar to those of Crittenden. These proposals were presented to Congress on 27 February, three days before the end of the session. They had little impact and were rejected by the Senate.

David Potter was correct when he observed that 'given the momentum of secession and the fundamental set of Republicanism, it is probably safe to say that compromise was impossible from the start'. The seven Confederate states had burned their bridges and had no wish to accept any compromise. The Republican party, determined not to give in to Southern blackmail, was also unwilling to compromise on the crucial issue of slavery expansion.

5 Lincoln's Position

Lord John Russell, the British Foreign Secretary, said in 1861, 'I do not see how the United States can be cobbled together again. The best thing now would be that the right to secede should be acknowledged'. This, however, was something that relatively few Northerners would accept. Up to 1860 slavery (or rather slavery expansion) had been the main issue dividing North from South. Secession, however, had now become the key issue. There were some Northerners who thought that the 'erring' Confederate states should be allowed to 'go in peace' and that their loss would be good riddance. But most Northerners regarded the Union as perpetual. Holding the view that the individual states had surrendered their independence on ratifying the Constitution after 1787, Northerners were not willing to accept the dismemberment of the United States. They feared that toleration of disunion in 1861 would create a fatal precedent to be invoked by disaffected minorities in the future, until the United States dissolved into a host of petty, squabbling nations. The great experiment in republican, self-government would thus collapse. 'The doctrine of secession is anarchy', declared a Cincinnati newspaper, echoing the views of hundreds of other Northern newspapers. 'If the minority have the right to break up the Government at pleasure, because they have not had their way, there is an end of all government'. The conclusion was that the North must stand firm and oppose secession.

However, few Republicans demanded the swift despatch of troops to suppress the Southern 'rebellion'. Some did not yet take the establishment of the Confederacy too seriously. Those who did take it seriously realised that precipitous action might have a disastrous impact on the upper South. They saw the advantage of making the seceded states appear to be preventing compromise. The best bet seemed to be to watch, wait and avoid needless provocation, hoping that the disunion fever would run its course and that the people of the lower South would see sense and return to the Union. In general Republican tactics in Congress were to do little and certainly give nothing away before Lincoln's inauguration.

Lincoln continued to maintain a strict silence. A prudent lawyer, he liked to weigh his options, seeking ways to balance contending opinions, before moving cautiously to attain his goals. He thought it best to wait until his inauguration, after which he would finally be in a position to take action. However, in a letter written on 1 February to William Seward (soon to be his Secretary of State), Lincoln made his views clear:

1 I say now ... as I have all the while said, that on the territorial question - that is, the question of extending slavery under the national auspices - I am inflexible. I am for no compromise which assists or permits the extension of the institution on soil owned by
5 the nation. And any trick by which the nation is to acquire territory, and then allow some local authority to spread slavery over it, is as obnoxious as any other. I take it that to effect some such result as this, and to put us again on the highroad to a slave empire,

is the object of all these proposed compromises. I am against it. As
10 to fugitive slaves, District of Columbia, slave trade among the slave
States and whatever springs of necessity from the fact that the
institution is amongst us, I care but little, save that what is done be
comely and not altogether outrageous. Nor do I care much about
15 New Mexico, if further extension were hedged against.

Lincoln, therefore, was ready to make a number of concessions. But,
New Mexico apart, he refused to budge on the territorial question. On
this, he was determined to 'hold firm as with a chain of steel'. He
believed that he and the Republicans had won the 1860 election on
principles fairly stated and was determined not to give too much away to
the slaveholders. 'If we surrender it is the end of us', he thought.

Like many Republicans, Lincoln exaggerated the strength of Union
feeling in the South: he thought - mistakenly - that secession was a plot
by a small but powerful group of wealthy planters. His hope that
masterly inactivity might allow Unionists in the South a chance to rally
and overthrow the extremists was naive. Nevertheless, in practical terms
this probably made little difference to the crisis. Even with hindsight, it
is difficult to see what Lincoln could have said or done before he was
inaugurated President which would have dramatically changed matters.

Over the winter of 1860-1, Lincoln was not only concerned with the
crisis in the South. He also had to select his cabinet. Given the crisis, he
wanted the best talent his party had to offer. But he also needed to satisfy
all the Republican factions, geographically, politically and ideologically.
The cabinet which he finally appointed was more a cabinet of all factions
than of all talents. Some of its members were radical, others
conservative. Some represented the East, others the West. (Lincoln
would have liked to appoint a 'real' Southerner but there was no obvious
candidate.) Some were former Whigs, others former Democrats. Four
of the seven men he appointed to cabinet posts had actually been fellow
competitors for the 1860 Republican nomination. Not one had been
friendly with Lincoln pre 1861: he knew little about them and, for the
most part, they knew even less about him.

Seward, the best known Republican in the country, was the obvious
choice for the most important post - Secretary of State. Eight years older
than Lincoln, he had been governor of New York, had served 12 years in
the Senate and knew everyone that mattered. Once considered a radical
by many Democrats, he was now increasingly 'conservative'. For several
weeks, he was the chief Republican in Washington, a position he
enjoyed. He expected - and was expected - to be the power behind the
throne. Salmon Chase, a former governor and Senator from Ohio,
became Secretary of the Treasury. He was seen as the main radical
spokesman in the cabinet. Gideon Welles, from Connecticut, became
Secretary of the Navy. The appointment of Caleb Smith, from Indiana,
as Secretary of the Interior and Simon Cameron, from Pennsylvania, as

Secretary of War were seen as 'debt' appointments in return for support for Lincoln's presidential nomination. The Attorney General Edward Bates came from Missouri while Montgomery Blair, the Postmaster General, came from Maryland. Some thought that Lincoln's cabinet appointments indicated his political naivety and doubted that he would have the personality to control such a disparate team. But Lincoln trusted to his political skill and powers of leadership to make the separate elements pull together.

Lincoln spent a great deal of time after his election deciding more basic patronage matters. He dealt patiently with the army of office seekers who came first to Springfield (and later to Washington) to plead for government jobs. Some thought this was time wasted: it was likened to Nero fiddling while Rome burned. But patronage matters were important for Republican party loyalty: party workers expected reward for their work. Ultimately Lincoln rewarded Republican supporters very well, removing Democrats from practically every office they held.

Lincoln finally set out from Springfield to Washington in mid-February. Instead of travelling directly to the capital, he went on a pre-inaugural tour, stopping off at various towns to show himself and to make set speeches. This was probably a mistake: he said little that was not trite or platitudinous - to the disappointment of many who heard him. Nearing Baltimore, Lincoln was warned of an assassination plot by his security advisers. Deciding to heed their advice, he abandoned his planned journey and slipped into Washington anonymously - 'like a thief in the night' according to his critics. This act, which seemed both cowardly and undignified and which embarrassed even Lincoln's most loyal supporters, cast doubts about his courage and firmness to face the crisis ahead. In addition, neither his gaunt, shambling appearance nor his Western accent and social awkwardness inspired much confidence. Nor did the fact that he had virtually no administrative experience and, unlike Jefferson Davis, was not trained to command. An outsider to Washington, (his last visit to the city had been twelve years earlier), he obviously needed time to acclimatise and also time to learn how to be President. But unfortunately time was a commodity he simply did not have.

The next few days were a nightmare. Lincoln met mobs of office seekers and endless delegations - Senators, Congressmen, delegates from the upper South, and important individuals like Buchanan, Douglas, and members of his own cabinet. Meanwhile, Lincoln worked hard on his inauguration speech. Aware that so much was at stake, he constantly revised and polished it. The speech was looked over by several people, including Seward who persuaded Lincoln to soften a few phrases and offer rather more in the way of concessions to the South.

On 4 March 1861 Lincoln was inaugurated President. His inaugural speech, which was particularly aimed at the upper South, was conciliatory but firm. He made it clear that he would not interfere with slavery where it already existed. Nor would he take immediate action to reclaim Federal property or appoint Federal officials in the South. But he also made it abundantly clear that, in his view, the Union was not dissoluble and that secession was illegal. Acts of violence against the authority of the United States would amount to insurrection and he declared he intended to 'hold, occupy and possess' Federal property within the seceded states and to collect 'duties and imposts'. He ended his speech with the following words (which owed something to Seward):

1 In your hands, my dissatisfied fellow countrymen, and not in mine, is the momentous issue of civil war. The government will not assail you. You can have no conflict without being yourselves the aggressors. You have no oath registered in heaven to destroy the
5 government, while I shall have the most solemn one to 'preserve, protect, and defend' it. I am loathe to close. We are not enemies, but friends. We must not be enemies. Though passion may have strained, it must not break, our bonds of affection. The mystic cords of memory, stretching from every battlefield and patriot
10 grave to every living heart and hearthstone all over this broad land, will yet swell the chorus of the Union when again touched, as surely they will be, by the better angels of our nature.

Some Democrat newspapers claimed that Lincoln's speech was incoherent, rambling and unscholarly. But most Republicans were pleased with Lincoln's firm tone. He promised to replace Buchanan's dithering with bold direction. Border state Unionists and many Northern Democrats were also pleased at his attempts at conciliation. Senator Douglas considered the speech a 'peace offering'. Unfortunately, the speech had no effect whatsoever in the Confederate states.

6 The Problem of Fort Sumter

Interestingly, given the crisis, Lincoln did not seek to keep Congress in session. Possibly this indicates that he still did not foresee Civil War. Certainly, as his inaugural speech indicated, he hoped that time might allow passions to cool. Within hours of becoming President, however, he was informed that time was not on his side. The situation at Fort Sumter called for a speedy decision.

Over the winter of 1860-1 the Confederacy had taken over all but a few forts and arsenals in the South. Most of the forts were unmanned except for a handful of maintenance personnel who offered no resistance. However, there were two exceptions: Fort Pickens and Fort Sumter. Both forts were on islands. Fort Pickens (off Pensacola, Florida) was well out of range of shore batteries and could easily be reinforced by the Federal navy. Fort Sumter, in the middle of Charleston harbour, was a far more serious problem. Over the winter and spring of 1861 everyone in America watched events unfold at Sumter.

The small Union force in Charleston was commanded by Major Robert Anderson. Anderson, an ex-Kentucky slave owner, had some sympathy for the South. Indeed, he had been chosen to command in Charleston by John Floyd, Buchanan's Southern Secretary of War, because he presumed he would act with Southern bias. However, Anderson determined to remain loyal to the flag he had served for 35 years. Once South Carolina seceded, Anderson, with no direct communication with Washington, faced a number of difficult decisions. With less than a hundred men under his command, he had to guard three military establishments - Fort Moultrie, Castle Pinckney and Fort Sumter. This was clearly an impossibility. Castle Pinckney was poorly armed and Fort Moultrie too big to defend properly. On the night of 26-27 December 1860, without specific orders from Buchanan, Anderson evacuated Fort Moultrie and concentrated his force at the unfinished but far more defensible Fort Sumter. Henceforward his main concern was to avoid any incident which might spark off war.

In January 1861 Buchanan sent a ship - the 'Star of the West' - with supplies and reinforcements for Anderson. But as the ship approached Sumter, South Carolina batteries opened fire and the 'Star of the West's captain hastily retreated. Anderson decided not to return fire and war in January was thus avoided. Secessionists from other states, worried by events, quietly warned South Carolina to cool down. They feared that the state's precipitous actions might provoke a conflict before the Confederacy was ready. The upshot was that a truce (of sorts) was agreed to allow time for negotiations between South Carolina and Washington.

By March 1861 Fort Sumter had become the symbol of national sovereignty for both sides. The Confederacy felt it could hardly allow a 'foreign' fort in the middle of Charleston harbour. Acquisition of the fort seemed essential if the Confederacy was to lay claim to the full rights of a sovereign nation. Lincoln had made it clear in his inauguration speech, that he was determined to hold on to what remained of Federal property in the South. Retention of Sumter was thus a test of the credibility of his government. Evacuation of the fort would be a sign of craven weakness. Yet Lincoln was also aware that firm action on his part might drive the upper South into secession.

Lincoln had spoken as he did at his inauguration, believing that time was on his side. But the day after his speech, he received a dispatch from Anderson which made it clear that the Sumter garrison only had four to six weeks supplies of food left. Lincoln knew that if he attempted to supply Sumter, this would probably be taken as a challenge by the Confederacy and might quickly lead to war. Lincoln had to reach a military decision and therefore sought the advice of his general-in-chief, 75 year old Winfield Scott. Scott, a native Virginian but totally loyal to the Union, had a towering military reputation, mainly earned during the Mexican War. Sumter's evacuation, he informed Lincoln, was 'almost inevitable': it could not be held without a large fleet and 25,000 soldiers, neither of which the United States possessed. On 15 March Lincoln brought the matter before his cabinet. Most favoured withdrawal. Only Blair stood firmly for an attempt to provision the fort. Lincoln put off making an immediate decision. In the meantime he sent trusted observers to Charleston to assess the situation.

Seward was the chief spokesmen for the policy of masterly inactivity. If the upper South was not stampeded into joining the Confederacy by a coercive act, Seward argued, the isolated Confederate states would have no choice but to rejoin the Union. Better informed than most Republicans of the situation in the South, he thought Lincoln should make some effort to appease the Confederacy. He realised that the outbreak of hostilities between the Federal government and the Confederacy would tend to unite the entire South and might divide the North. While Lincoln prevaricated, Seward, acting on his own initiative, sent assurances to Confederate leaders, through a series of intermediaries, that Sumter would be abandoned. Confederate leaders, while not altogether trusting the devious Seward, presumed he was speaking on behalf of the President.

At the end of March, following a report from Scott which declared that Sumter and Pickens should both be abandoned, Lincoln called another cabinet meeting to discuss the crisis. By now, his fact-finding mission to Charleston had returned and reported that they could find no Unionist feeling whatsoever: the hope that Unionist sentiment would ultimately prevail was thus demolished. More important, there was a clamour in the North (especially in newspapers) for firm action and for not abandoning Sumter. Heedful of this clamour, the cabinet rejected Scott's advice. A majority now spoke in favour of resupplying Sumter and all favoured protecting Pickens. Lincoln made it clear that he would give orders for an expedition to sail to Sumter and Pickens to reprovision, but not reinforce, the forts.

Seward, who had thought the evacuation of Sumter a foregone conclusion, had clearly miscalculated. Still trying to control the situation and maintain his credibility in the South, he sent Lincoln a memorandum in which he suggested that Lincoln should delegate power to himself, evacuate Sumter and provoke a war against France and Spain which might help to re-unite the nation. Lincoln showed remarkable restraint in his response. (Indeed he probably never sent an official response: he had more important things to do than exchange memos with a colleague, whom he had appointed, about who was in charge.) But he made it clear to Seward that he had no intention of delegating power, of abandoning Sumter or of fighting more than one war at a time.

On 4 April Lincoln informed Anderson that a relief expedition would soon be coming and that he should try to hold out until supplies reached him. Two days later Lincoln sent a letter to Governor Pickens of South Carolina telling him that he intended to re-supply Sumter. Some confusion then ensued. At Seward's instigation, the warship 'Powhaton' set off (with an order, mistakenly signed by Lincoln) to reprovision Fort Pickens. Lincoln believed that the ship was on its way to Sumter. In consequence, it was not until 9 April that a small naval expedition - 3 ships and some 500 men - finally left for Charleston.

Some historians think that Lincoln deliberately and cynically manoeuvred the Confederacy into firing the first shots. Others believe that his main concern in attempting to resupply Sumter was to try to preserve the status quo and give himself - and the Confederacy - more time. In reality, it seems likely that Lincoln was trying to keep as many options open as possible. He hoped to preserve peace, but was willing to risk war. By determining to re-supply Sumter, he was lobbing the ball into Jefferson Davis's court. The Confederacy now had to decide what to do. If Confederate leaders gave the orders to fire on unarmed boats carrying food for hungry men, they would clearly be in the wrong. At the very least this would unite Northern opinion and might well affect the border states.

On 9 April Davis called a cabinet meeting. Toombs, his Secretary of State, opposed taking action against Sumter, arguing that this would only serve to unite the North. But Toombs was a lone voice. Most of the Confederate cabinet thought that the time had come to lance the Sumter boil. The fact that the Stars and Stripes was still flying on the fort was an affront to Southern honour. Moreover, a crisis might unite the whole South and bring the border states into the Confederacy. Davis, in tune with his cabinet, issued orders that Sumter must be taken before it was resupplied. General Pierre Beauregard, the commander of the Confederate forces in Charleston, was to demand that Anderson immediately evacuate the fort. If Anderson refused, then Beauregard's orders were to 'reduce' Sumter. In Alan Nevin's view, this was 'an act of rash emotionalism'. The Confederacy was precipitating a conflict for which it was ill-prepared and which was to seal its doom.

On 11 April Beauregard, obeying orders, demanded the immediate surrender of Sumter. Anderson (who had once been Beauregard's tutor and at West Point) refused. He pointed out that lack of food would force him to surrender in a few days anyway. Negotiations dragged on for several hours but got nowhere. And so, at 4.30 am on 12 April 1861, the opening shots of the Civil War were fired. For 33 hours the defenders of Sumter exchanged artillery fire with Confederate batteries on land. Some 5,000 rounds were fired: 3,500 by the Confederate forces; 1,500 by Sumter's defenders. The extraordinary thing was that there were no fatalities. The naval relief expedition arrived too late - and was too small - to effect proceedings. On 13 April, with fires raging through Fort Sumter, Anderson felt he had done his duty. Terms of surrender were quickly arranged and the following day Anderson's troops marched out, with colours flying and were evacuated to Washington. The South had gained a military victory - but a victory that was ultimately far more disastrous than any of its later military defeats.

On 15 April Lincoln issued a Call to Arms. It was clear that the attack on Fort Sumter had electrified the North. In New York, a city which had previously tended to be pro-Southern, 250,000 people turned out for a Union rally. Northerners were ready to fight; less to abolish slavery than to punish secession. 'There can be no neutrals in this war, only patriots - or traitors', thundered Senator Douglas. Neither Lincoln nor the Confederacy expected a long conflict. Lincoln asked for 75,000 men for 90 days: Davis called for 100,000 men. Such was the enthusiasm that both sides were inundated with troops. Northern governors complained that they had ten times the number Lincoln asked for. Lincoln insisted that he was dealing with a rebellion and that this was not a war. Nevertheless, on 19 April he ordered a blockade of the Confederacy. This implied that the conflict was more a war than a rebellion.

7 Secession: The Second Wave

Given that Lincoln called on all Union states to send men to put down the Confederate 'rebellion', the upper South states had to commit themselves. Virginia's decision was crucial. The oldest state in America, it had considerable prestige. More important, it had an industrial capacity as great as the seven original Confederate states combined. If Virginia opted to remain in the Union, it was unlikely that the Confederacy had much chance of survival. But there was never much doubt about the way that Virgina would vote. Most Virginians sympathised with the Confederacy. Delighted by the capture of Fort Sumter and angered by the North's aggressive actions, the state voted by 88 votes to 55 to support its Southern 'brothers'. (A referendum in May ratified the convention's decision, with Virginians voting 128,884 votes to 32,134 to secede from the Union.) In May the Provisional Congress in Montgomery elected to make Richmond the Confederate capital, a move designed to cement the Virginian alliance.

In May Arkansas and North Carolina joined the Confederacy. In June Tennessee voted by 104,913 votes to 47,238 to secede. Many people in these states were reluctant secessionists. A former Whig Senator Jonathan Worth from North Carolina, who had opposed secession until it became a fait accompli, wrote: 'I think the annals of the world furnish no instance of so groundless a war but as our nation will have it - if no peace can be made - let us fight like men for our firesides'.

Support for the Confederacy in the upper South was far from total. West Virginia now effectively seceded from Virginia and remained in the Union. East Tennessee did likewise. There were significant pockets of Union support in North Carolina and Arkansas. Even more important, four slave states - Delaware, Maryland, Missouri, and Kentucky - decided to remain within the Union. There was never any likelihood of Delaware seceding. Only 2 per cent of its population were slaves and the state was strongly pro-Union. Maryland seemed more likely to join the Confederacy: it had voted for Breckinridge in 1860 and state rights Democrats controlled its legislature. Large numbers of Marylanders, especially in Baltimore, initially supported the Confederacy. On 19 April troops from Massachusetts on the way to defend Washington were attacked by the Baltimore mob and were forced to open fire. Four soldiers and twelve civilians were killed. But fortunately for Lincoln, Maryland's Governor Hicks remained loyal to the Union. Lincoln took firm action, suspending habeas corpus and arresting a number of suspected rebels. Elections to Congress in June were won by Unionist candidates and, even though large numbers of Marylanders fought for the Confederacy, the state remained in the Union. Missouri was similarly divided. But firm action by Union supporters prevented the pro-Southern Governor taking the state into the Confederacy. Kentucky, the birthplace of Lincoln and Davis, was vital for both sides. Its population seems to have been equally divided in its loyalties. The state government tried to remain neutral but an unwise invasion by Confederate troops in September 1861 resulted in Kentucky deciding to remain in the Union. Had Maryland, Kentucky and Missouri joined the Confederacy, this would have added 45 per cent to its white population and 80 per cent to its manufacturing capacity. The Civil War might then have had a very different conclusion.

8 Conclusion

Did a blundering set of politicians fail to find an obvious solution to the crisis? The answer I think is partly no - and partly yes. Even with the benefit of hindsight, it is difficult to see what compromise measures might have persuaded the Confederate states to return to the Union. In consequence, it is unfair to blame Lincoln and the Republican party. Lincoln, was prepared to make some important concessions. It was Confederate leaders who refused to compromise. Those same leaders ordered the attack on Fort Sumter. This action was as desperate and as suicidal as the Japanese attack on Pearl Harbour 80 years later. Southern politicians had blundered into war: it was a blunder that the 260,000 Southerners who died in the Civil War would not live to regret.

Making notes on 'The Outbreak of Civil War'

Your notes on this chapter should give you an understanding of the process by which the establishment of the Confederacy led to Civil War. Your notes should help you answer the following questions:

1 Why did the upper South states not secede during the winter of 1860-1?
2 Could and should a compromise have been found in 1860-1?
3 How well did Abraham Lincoln handle events from November 1860 to April 1861?
4 Was Lincoln intent on war by April 1861?

Answering essay questions on 'The Outbreak of Civil War'

Questions for this (limited time-scale) period are likely to focus on whether the politicians, both in the North and in the South, stumbled into war. To be able to provide a well-rounded answer you will need to include information not just from this chapter but also from the previous chapters and the next one. Here are two examples of possible questions:

1 'Compromise between North and South could and should have been found over the winter of 1860-1'. Discuss.
2. Should Lincoln be praised or blamed for his handling of events from his election in November 1860 to the firing of the first shots at Fort Sumter in April 1861?

Both questions deal with many of the same issues but each will have a different focus. In question 1 you will need to examine the attempts at compromise that were made in 1860-1. Did foolish Northern politicians fail to find an obvious solution to the crisis (as the quote implies) or had North and South become so divided by 1860 that compromise was impossible? You will have realised by now that I support the latter view. In consequence, I would attack the quote. But I would argue that Southern leaders were foolish not to seek a compromise and get as good a deal as they could from Lincoln - who was prepared to make some concessions (which might well have divided his party - to the South's advantage). My opinion should not necessarily influence you. Historians like to claim that nothing in history is inevitable. If that is true, then obviously a case can be made for blundering politicians. What is also true is that American politicians in 1860-1 did not have the historian's benefit of hindsight. Few expected a long war. If either side had been aware of the kind of war they were about to unleash, greater efforts might have been made to reach a solution. (Note that the fact that the leading men failed to appreciate the horrors ahead can also be used in evidence against them.) Brainstorm the main arguments you might make in support of the quote in the question. Then list the main arguments against the quote. Which set of arguments do you find most convincing and why? Your ideas are worth jotting down: they should form the basis of a good conclusion to the essay.

Question 2 is much more focussed on Abraham Lincoln. But much of the 'meat' of this essay is similar to that in question 1. If compromise was impossible, then it is somewhat unfair to blame Lincoln. However, if compromise was a real possibility, then Lincoln must be put in the 'dock', along with the other blundering politicians in both the North and the South. Write down a possible introductory paragraph and a possible conclusion for question 2.

Source-based questions on 'The Outbreak of Civil War'

1 Lincoln's letter to Seward
Read the extract from Lincoln's letter to Seward in February 1861 on page 133-4. Answer the following questions:
a) Why exactly was Lincoln writing to Seward in February 1861?
   (5 marks)
b) Why is this source of great importance to historians? (5 marks)
c) How might it be possible to check whether Lincoln was taking a consistent stance or changing ground as the situation changed?
   (5 marks)

2 Lincoln's Inaugural Address
Read the extract from Lincoln's inaugural speech on page 136. Answer the following questions:
a) What were Lincoln's main motives when making his inaugural address? (5 marks)
b) Comment on Lincoln's statement: 'In your hands, my dissatisfied fellow countrymen, and not in mine, is the momentous issue of civil war'. (5 marks)
c) What did Lincoln mean when he spoke of the 'mystic cords of memory'? (5 marks)

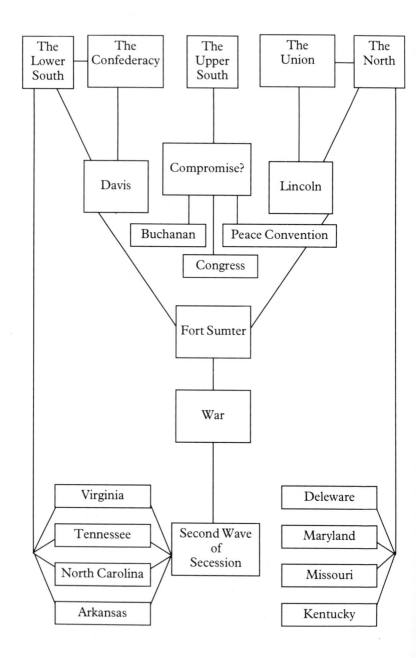

Summary - The Outbreak of Civil War

CHAPTER 9

The Causes of the Civil War: Conclusion

1 The Main Historiographical Debates

Few subjects have been more keenly debated than what caused the Civil War. In March 1865 Abraham Lincoln, in his second inaugural address, presented one of the most succinct explanations of how and why the war came:

1 On the occasion corresponding this four years ago all thoughts were anxiously directed to an impending civil war. All dreaded it, all sought to avert it. While the inaugural address was being delivered from this place, devoted altogether to saving the Union
5 without war, insurgent agents were in the city seeking to destroy it without war - seeking to dissolve the Union and divide effects by negotiation. Both parties deprecated war, but one of them would make war rather than let the nation survive, and the other would accept war rather than let it perish, and the war came.

One eighth of the whole population was coloured slaves, not distributed generally over the Union, but localised in the southern part of it. These slaves constituted a peculiar and powerful interest. All knew that this interest was somehow the cause of the war. To strengthen, perpetuate, and extend this interest was the object for which the insurgents would rend the Union even by war, while the government claimed no right to do more than to restrict the territorial enlargement of it.

Slavery, in Lincoln's view, was thus 'somehow' the cause of the war. For 50 years after the war, few Northern historians dissented from this opinion. In 1913 James Ford Rhodes, the foremost Civil War historian of his day, declared that 'of the American Civil War it may safely be asserted that there was a single cause, slavery'. But there were historians then - and there have been many since - who would have disagreed strongly with this view. Indeed the Confederate leaders Jefferson Davis and Alexander Stephens both insisted in their memoirs that Southern states had seceded and gone to war not to protect slavery but to vindicate state sovereignty. Davis, writing in the 1870s, insisted that the Confederates had fought solely 'for the defence of an inherent, unalienable right ... to withdraw from a Union which they had, as sovereign communities, voluntarily entered ... The existence of African servitude was in no wise the cause of the conflict, but only an incident'. This explanation was accepted by many Southerners who thus continued to view the conflict as a war of Northern aggression against Southern rights.

In the 1920s many historians believed clashes between interest groups and classes underpinned most events in history. The war, in the eyes of some 'progressive' historians, was a contest between plantation agriculture, on the one hand, and industrialising capitalism on the other. It was not primarily a conflict between North and South: 'Merely by the accidents of climate, soil and geography was it a sectional struggle', wrote Charles Beard, the leading progressive historian. Nor, in Beard's view, was the war a contest between slavery and freedom. Slavery just happened to be the labour system of plantation agriculture, just as wage labour happened to be the system of Northern industry. For some progressive historians, neither system was significantly worse or better than the other. In any case, they said, slavery was not a moral issue for anybody except a tiny handful of abolitionists. The real issues between Northern manufacturers and Southern planters before the war were, according to Beard and other progressives, the tariff, government subsidies to transportation and manufacturing, and public land sales.

Many Southern historians were delighted with this. The Confederacy, it seemed, fought not only for the principle of state rights and self-government but also for the preservation of a stable, agrarian civilisation in the face of the grasping ambitions of Northern businessmen. Perhaps it was no coincidence that this interpretation emerged at much the same period that 'Gone With the Wind' became one of the most popular literary and cinematic successes of all time.

During the 1940s another interpretation, usually called 'revisionism' came to dominate the work of academic historians. The revisionists denied that sectional conflicts between North and South - whether over slavery, state rights, or industry versus agriculture - were genuinely divisive. In the view of the two revisionist 'giants' Avery Craven and James Randall, far more united than divided the two sections. The free and slave states had coexisted peacefully under the same Constitution since 1787. White Americans shared the same language, legal system, political culture, racial views, religious values and a common heritage. In the eyes of the revisionists, the differences that separated North and South could have been accommodated peacefully. Compromise should have been found. The Civil War was, therefore, not an irrepressible conflict, as earlier generations had called it, but 'The Repressible Conflict', as Craven titled one of his books. The war was brought on not by genuine issues but by extremists on both sides - rabble-rousing abolitionists and Southern fire-eaters - who whipped up emotions and hatreds for their own partisan purposes. The passions they aroused got out of hand because politicians of the time lacked the skill of previous generations and failed to find a compromise. The result was a tragic, unnecessary war that accomplished nothing that could not have been achieved by negotiation. Of course, any compromise in 1860-1 would have left slavery in place. But revisionists argued that slavery would have died peacefully of natural causes in another generation or two.

Revisionists tended to focus most of their criticism on anti-slavery radicals who harped on the evils of slavery and expressed a determination to destroy the Slave Power. This, in the opinion of some revisionists, goaded the South into a defensive response that finally caused Southern states to secede.

2 The Importance of Slavery

Since the 1950s, however, historiography has come full circle. Most historians now agree with Lincoln's assertion that slavery was 'somehow' the cause of the war. The state rights, progressive, and revisionist schools are presently dormant if not actually dead. Most historians, while accepting that the agricultural South and the industrialising North did have different economic interests, believe that the Civil War was not fought over issues such as the tariff or banks or agrarianism versus industrialism. Such issues have existed throughout American history, often generating a great deal more friction than they did in the 1850s. Nor do most historians today think the war was the result of false issues trumped up by Northern or Southern fanatics. Instead they believe it was fought over profound, intractable problems that went to the heart of mid-nineteenth century American society - and its future. Slavery lay at the root of the antagonism. To say that 'only' slavery divided the North from the South is akin to saying that 'only' religion divides people in Northern Ireland. Slavery was the sole institution not shared by North and South. It defined the South, permeating almost every aspect of its life. In 1858 William Seward voiced the stark nature of the problem. The social systems of slave labour and free labour 'are more than incongruous - they are incompatible', said Seward. The friction between them is 'an irreconcilable conflict between opposing and enduring forces, and it means that the United States must and will, sooner or later, become entirely a slaveholding nation, or entirely a free-labour nation'. By the 1850s Southern spokesmen agreed with Seward that the country had been split into two hostile, irreconcilable cultures. Many Southerners had come to the view that, because of the Northern threat to slavery, they should secede from a Union controlled by the North.

Slaves were the principal form of wealth in the South. The market value of the South's 4,000,000 slaves in 1860 was $3 billion - more than the value of land and cotton. But slavery was much more than an economic system. It was a means of maintaining racial control and white supremacy. Northern whites were also committed to white supremacy. But with 95 per cent of the nation's black population in the South, the region's scale of concern with this matter was so much greater as to constitute a different order of magnitude. Only 25 per cent of Southern whites actually owned slaves in 1860. But the vast majority of non-slaveholding whites supported slavery. Many aspired to become slaveholders themselves. Most feared what would happen if the slaves were freed. Slavery seemed essential to the peace, safety and prosperity of the South.

The rise of militant abolitionism in the North after 1830 exacerbated tension between the sections. William Lloyd Garrison, Frederick Douglas and a host of other eloquent crusaders branded slavery as both a sin and a violation of the republican principles of liberty on which the USA had been founded. Although the abolitionists did not get far in the North with their message of racial equality, the belief that slavery was unjust, obsolete and unrepublican, entered mainstream Northern politics. Slavery was seen as degrading the concept of labour, and impoverishing poor and middling whites who could not compete with slave planters. But it was the issue of slavery expansion, rather than the mere existence of slavery, that polarised the nation. Most of the crises that threatened the bonds of Union arose over this matter: the 1819-20 Missouri crisis; the problem of the Mexican territories after 1846; and finally events in Kansas after 1854. Convinced that a Slave Power conspiracy was at work, Northerners ultimately came to support the Republican Party, which was pledged to stop slavery expansion and defeat the Slave Power.

The breakdown of the second party system and the voter realignment of the 1850s had more to do - at least initially - with nativist issues than slavery. It was the Know Nothings rather than the Republicans who ruined the Whigs and reduced Democrat strength in the North. But ultimately it was the Republican party which emerged as the main anti-Democrat party. The success of the Republican party in the late 1850s was a crucial step to war. For many Southerners the election of the Republican Abraham Lincoln as President in 1860 was the last straw. The election demonstrated that the South was increasingly a minority region within the nation. The fact that the government was now to be controlled by a man who believed that slavery 'should be placed in the course of ultimate extinction' was an affront to Southern honour. So, the lower South seceded.

3 Nationalism

In 1861 Lincoln was not pledged to end slavery: he was pledged to preserve the Union. The Confederate states were fighting for the right to self-determination. Thus nationalism became in 1861 the central issue of the struggle on both sides. Historians continue to debate the extent to which the South, in particular, had a national identity in 1861. It is not easy to measure nationalism's precise ingredients: it is a matter of sentiment and loyalty. By the mid-nineteenth century there were certainly Southerners who fervently believed in a separate Southern destiny and who hoped to bring about the creation of a Southern nation. Their rhetoric became part of the common political discourse: perhaps they made secession and Southern independence thinkable. Some have claimed that the ante-bellum South did possess the cultural conditions necessary for the development of a sense of separate nationhood. It is possible, for example, to claim that the South had an ethnic and religious homogeneity that marked it off from the North. Ethnically (if one ignores the presence of some 4,000,000 African Americans!) the South was more homogeneous than the North. Most Southern whites were of British descent: there were relatively few Irish or German immigrants. Most Southerners, therefore, were Protestants: there were few Catholics. Southern nationalists also manufactured (imaginary) ethnic differences. White Southerners were told that they were descended from - gentlemanly and civilised - Cavaliers. Northerners, on the other hand, were held to be descended from - ungentlemanly and uncivilised - Roundheads. The Cavalier-Roundhead distinction was a myth. Nevertheless many believed it and it was thus important.

However, most of the things that united Southern whites were shared by most other Americans. Most Northerners were of British stock. Most were Protestant. Before 1860, there had been little enthusiasm for creating a Southern nation. Most Southerners had seen themselves as loyal Americans. The Southern fire-eaters were a small minority. They did not obtain high office either before - or indeed after - 1861. Most Southerners considered them cranks and fanatics. Many of those who advocated secession during the winter of 1860-1 did so reluctantly. The establishment of the Confederacy was a refuge to which many Southerners felt driven, not a national destiny that they eagerly embraced. Arguably the Civil War did more to produce Southern nationalism than Southern nationalism did to produce war. In so far as there was a sense of Southern nationalism in 1860-1, it had arisen because of slavery. The peculiar institution set the South apart from the rest of the nation - and indeed from most of the rest of the world. Slavery was the interest that Southern politicians most wished to defend.

Northern nationalism must also be considered. Secession by the Confederate states might not necessarily have led to war. It would have been feasible for the North to have simply let the Southern states go. But most Northerners were not prepared to accept this. Instead they preferred to fight. Most Northerners did not go to war to end slavery. Emancipation did not become a Union war aim until 1862. In fact, as late as September 1862 Lincoln proclaimed: 'If I could save the Union without freeing any slaves I would do it, and if I could save it by freeing all the slaves, I would do it, and if I could save it by freeing some and leaving others alone I would also do that'. For Lincoln, and for most Northerners, the war was essentially about saving the Union and maintaining the great experiment. (Few saw irony in the fact that before - and after - 1861 the USA consistently supported the struggles of peoples elsewhere in the world for self-determination.) Almost all the young men who flocked to join the Union armies in 1861 were swept along on an emotional wave of nationalism.

Although few Northerners in 1861 were fighting to emancipate the slave, it was slavery which had led to the sectional impasse between North and South. It was differences arising from the slavery issue that impelled the Southern states to secede. There was a fear that a rampant North would destroy the Old South. As one South Carolinian put it: 'she will ride over us rough-shod, proclaim freedom, or something equivalent to it to our slaves and reduce us to the condition of Haiti ... If we do not act now, we deliberately consign our children, not our posterity, but our children to the flames'. While the Confederacy might claim its justification to be the protection of state rights, in truth, it was primarily one state right - the right to preserve slavery - that impelled the Confederate states' separation. For this right many Southerners were prepared to fight to the death.

Slavery underpinned the nationalist struggle. Slavery was the obvious difference between the two sections. It made the South distinct: it was, as Alexander Stephens said, the 'cornerstone' of the Confederacy. It was the main reason for the growth of sectionalism. It led to both sides stressing the cultural differences, which did exist but which were exaggerated. It led to Northerners stereo-typing Southerners as backward, semi-civilised reactionaries or sinners. It led to Southerners in turn viewing Northerners as abolitionists and revolutionaries. Slavery even underpinned the cultural differences. No other issue could have led to the disruption of the Union.

4 Who was to Blame?

With the advantage of hindsight, it is obvious that Southern politicians - and there is no doubt that they were representing the views of most white Southerners - got things wrong in 1860-1. They perceived that slavery was threatened and that 'Black Republican' revolution was about to engulf the South. This was a serious misconception. The peculiar institution was not in immediate peril. Lincoln thought it would be a hundred years or more before slavery withered and died. Southerners should have accepted the outcome of the democratic process: they should have accepted Northern dominance just as Northerners felt they had to bear Southern dominance for most of the 1850s. Given that the Republicans did not have a majority in Congress in 1860, there was little Lincoln could do to threaten slavery immediately. Indeed, he was prepared to make - substantial - concessions to the South: concessions which might have weakened his position in the North. From November 1860 to April 1861 Lincoln acted reasonably and rationally. The same cannot be said for Southerners and their leaders. Southerners did not have to secede. The desire to maintain slavery - which was rational - did not require the establishment of an independent Southern nation. Many slavery advocates believed that the peculiar institution would best be protected within the Union - and events proved them right.

For much of the antebellum period most Southern white people seem to have regarded the vocal Southern nationalists as quasi-lunatics. Unfortunately, the emotionally-charged atmosphere of 1859-61 ensured that lunatic ideas - not so much the lunatics themselves - took over the South. Secession was a reckless decision - an affair of passion. Some Southerners at the time realised the enormity of the mistake. They saw that secession would mean war - and that war probably would result in Confederate defeat and the end of slavery. The North Carolinian Jonathan Worth said in the spring of 1861: 'I think the South is committing suicide, but my lot is cast with the South and being unable to manage the ship, I intend to face the breakers manfully and go down with my companions'.

Historians can explain - and understand - the reasons why Southerners acted as they did. They are also entitled to pass judgement on those actions. Southerners in 1860-1 - politicians and electorate alike - made a series of horrendous blunders. Emotion got the better of most Southerners. The result was that most went enthusiastically to war - a war in which one in four white Southern men of military age died. There is undoubtedly some romance and glory in the South's 'Lost Cause' struggle. But that struggle was always likely to be a 'Lost Cause'. As Napoleon recognised, victory in war invariably goes to the side with the 'big battalions'. The North was so much stronger in terms of both men and industrial strength that it was always likely to win a Civil War. This was obvious to most Northerners: the fact that it was not obvious to most Southerners is symptomatic of the hysteria that swept the South in 1860-1. Southerners picked the quarrel. They fired the first shots at Fort Sumter - thus provoking a conflict for which the Confederacy was ill-prepared, and - at the same time - uniting the North. Irrationally and irresponsibly, they embarked on a war that from their point of view was - and was always likely to be - catastrophic.

Working on *'The Causes of the Civil War: Conclusion'*

This chapter reconsiders some of the issues raised in Chapter 1 and assesses why the American Civil War occurred. What was the main cause of the war? Was the war repressible? Who was to blame? These are issues which will continue to be debated. Different historians have different views. I have no doubt that slavery - particularly problems arising from slavery expansion - led ultimately to Civil War. Had the South acted rationally in 1860-1 war would not have occurred. But the odds were that Southerners would be carried away on a tidal wave of emotion. There need not have been war: but it is difficult to see how war could have been averted. In my view Southerners were mainly to blame for the crisis - and I am quite happy to use the word 'blame'. This does not necessarily mean that you should be. Nor should you automatically accept the views expressed in this chapter. You need to formulate your own judgements - and now is the time to do so. Think about the following essay title:

> To what extent should Southerners be held responsible for the outbreak of the American Civil War?

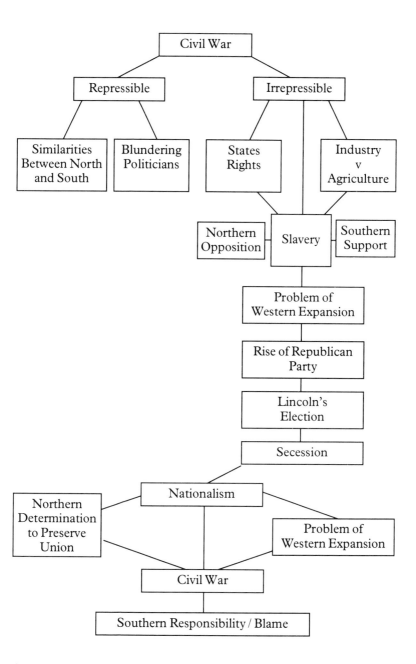

Summary - The Causes of the Civil War: Conclusion

Chronological Table

1820	February	Missouri Compromise
1831	January	Publication of *The Liberator*
	August	Nat Turner's revolt
1832-3		Nullification Crisis
1835	December	Texas declared independence from Mexico
1836	March	Mexicans captured the Alamo
	April	Battle of San Jacinto: Texas won independence
1841	March	Whig William Harrison inaugurated President
	April	President Harrison died. Vice President Tyler became President
1845	February	Congress adopted joint resolution for annexation of Texas
	March	Democrat James Polk inaugurated President
1846	February	Mormon migration westward led by Brigham Young
	May	Start of Mexican War
	June	Republic of California proclaimed
	August	Wilmot Proviso.
1847	February	Battle of Buena Vista. General Taylor defeated Santa Anna
	March	General Scott captured Vera Cruz.
	September	General Scott occupied Mexico City
1848	January	Gold discovered in California
	February	Treaty of Guadalupe Hidalgo
	July	American women's convention at Seneca Falls
1849	March	Whig Zachary Taylor inaugurated President
	November	California free state constitution ratified
1850	January	Henry Clay introduced Compromise bill
	July	Millard Fillmore became President on death of Taylor
	September	Compromise measures all passed
1851	June	*Uncle Tom's Cabin* began to appear in serial form
1853	March	Democrat Franklin Pierce inaugurated President
	December	Gadsden Purchase
1854	January	Introduction of Kansas-Nebraska Bill
	May	Kansas-Nebraska Act passed.
	October	Ostend Manifesto

1855	March	Election in Kansas: pro-slavery legislature
	September	Creation of free soil government in Kansas
1856	May	Pro-slavery force 'sacked' Lawrence
	May	Charles Sumner beaten by Preston Brooks
	May	John Brown killed 5 pro-slavers settlers at Pottawatomie
1857	March	Democrat James Buchanan inaugurated President
	August	Start of 'Panic of 1857'
	October	Free state legislature elected in Kansas
	December	Pro-slavery Lecompton Constitution adopted
1858	January	Senator Douglas split with President Buchanan
	June	Abraham Lincoln nominated as Republican Senator in Illinois
	August	Start of Lincoln-Douglas debates
	November	Douglas returned as Senator for Illinois
1859	October	John Brown raid on Harper's Ferry
	December	John Brown executed
1860	November	Abraham Lincoln elected President
	December	South Carolina seceded
1861	January	Mississippi, Florida, Alabama, Georgia and Louisiana seceded
	January	Kansas admitted to Union as 34th (free) state
	February	Establishment of the Confederacy
	February	Jefferson Davis became Confederate President
	February	Texas seceded.
	March	Lincoln inaugurated President
	April	Confederate forces open fire on Fort Sumter
	April	Lincoln declared state of 'insurrection'
	April	Virginia seceded
	April	First casualties of Civil War in Baltimore riot
	May	Arkansas and North Carolina seceded
	May	Richmond became Confederate capital
	June	Tennessee seceded

Further Reading

You will not be surprised to learn that there are hundreds of excellent books on the causes of the American Civil War, including some of the finest works of American history ever written. This list offers only a brief sample of some of the most significant works. It is unlikely that you will have time to consult more than just a few of these. However, it is vital that you read some, particularly if you are taking the topic as a special or depth study. The topic is one of considerable controversy and you will be in a better position to form your own conclusions if you have read widely. The following suggestions are meant to serve as a guide.

1 General texts

There are many general works that cover all or most of the period 1846 to 1861 (and beyond). These include:
J.M. McPherson, *Battle Cry of Freedom,* (Penguin 1988) - the best one-volume survey of the causes and course of the Civil War. **R.M. Sewell,** *A House Divided: Sectionalism and Civil War, 1848-1865,* (John Hopkins University Press 1988) - a shorter and more succinct account. **P.J. Parish,** *The American Civil War,* (Holmes and Meier 1975) - mainly concerned with the actual war but the first few chapters are worth reading. **D.M. Potter,** *The Impending Crisis 1846-61,* (Harper and Row 1976) - still an essential text. **R. Ransom,** *Conflict and Compromise: The Political Economy of Slavery, Emancipation and the American Civil War,* (Cambridge University Press 1989) - an excellent introduction. **B. Collins,** *The Origins of America's Civil War,* (Arnold 1981) - still worth reading. **A. Nevins,** *The Ordeal of the Union* (2 vols Charles Scribner's Sons 1947) and *The Emergence of the Union* (2 vols Charles Scribner's Sons 1950) - excellent but probably too detailed for most readers. **K.M. Stampp,** *The Imperiled Union: Essays on the Civil War Era,* (Oxford University Press 1980) - containing some valuable insights. Given that many of these books cover more than just the coming of the war, only the first section of most of them is likely to be relevant.

2 The USA in the Mid-nineteenth Century

Numerous texts cover political, economic and social aspects of American life in the early/mid-nineteenth century. On the political front it is worth reading: **M.F. Holt,** *Political Parties and American Political Developments from the Age of Jackson to the Age of Lincoln,* (Louisiana State University Press 1992). **C. Sellers,** *The Market Revolution: Jacksonian America 1815-1846,* (Oxford University Press 1991) provides a sweeping political and social history of American history pre-1846. On the economic front read: **D.C. North,** *The Economic Growth of the*

United States, (Norton 1966). **G.R. Taylor,** *The Transportation Revolution, 1815-1860,* (M.E. Sharpe Inc.1961) which covers not only transport but all aspects of economic life except farming. **P.W. Gates,** *The Farmer's Age, 1815-1860, (M.E. Sharpe Inc.1960)* deals with agriculture in the period. **T. Cochran,** *Frontiers of Change,* (Oxford University Press 1981) offers a brief survey of American economic development in the early 19th century. On the social side, try: **C Clinton,** *The Other Civil War,* (Hill and Wang 1984) which surveys the changing role of women in 19th century America. On the social side, **read: B. Collins,** *White Society in the Ante-bellum South* (Longman 1985). **B. Wyatt-Brown,** *Southern Honor: Ethics and Behaviour in the Old South,* (Oxford Papaerbacks 1982) which stresses the importance of honour in the *ante-bellum* South. **R. Carwardine,** *Transatlantic Revivalism: Popular Evangelism in Britain and America, 1790-1865,* (Greenwood Press 1978). **R.G. Walters,** *American Reformers, 1815-1860,* (Hill and Wang 1978) - a concise and informative introduction to this area.

3 The Peculiar Institution

Perhaps the best place to start is: **P.J. Parish,** *Slavery: History and Historians,* (Icon Editions 1989). This provides a splendid overview of the main debates. **K.M. Stampp,** *The Peculiar Institution: Slavery in the Ante-bellum South,* (Eyre and Spottiswoode 1956) remains essential. So does: **S.M. Elkins,** *Slavery: A Problem in American Institutional and Intellectual Life,* (University of Chicago Press 1959). **R.W. Fogel and S.L. Engerman,** *Time on the Cross: The Economics of American Negro Slavery,* (University Press of America 1974) has been slammed by umpteen critics and must be treated with care. **R.W. Fogel,** *Without Consent or Contract: The Rise and Fall of American Slavery,* (Norton1989) is an impressive work because it addresses the the moral questions ignored in *Time on the Cross.* **J.W. Blassingame,** *The Slave Community: Plantation Life in the Antebellum South,* (Oxford University Press 1979) examines slave conditions. As does: **H.G. Gutman,** *The Black Family in Slavery and Freedom 1750-1925,* (Random 1976). **R.B. Campbell,** *An Empire for Slavery: The Peculiar Institution in Texas 1821-65,* (Louisiana State University Press 1989) brilliantly examines slavery in Texas. **J. Oakes,** *The Ruling Race: A History of American Slaveholders,* (Vintage Books 1982) looks at the attitudes of white Southerners. **M.L. Dillon,** *The Abolitionists: The Growth of a Dissenting Minority,* (Norton 1974) is a reasonable introduction to the abolitionist movement. **J.B. Stewart,** *Holy Warriors: The Abolitionists and American Slavery,* (Hill and Wang 1976) is also worth reading.

4 The Problem of Western Expansion

R.A Billington, *The Far Western Frontier, 1830-1860,* (Harper and Row

1956) provides an excellent introduction to Western expansion. **T.R. Hietala,** *Manifest Destiny: Anxious Aggrandizement in Late Jacksonian America,* (Cornell University Press 1990) examines American motives for expansion. **R.W. Johannsen,** *To the Halls of the Montezumas: The Mexican War in the American Imagination,* (Oxford University Press 1988) examines the impact of the Mexican War on American opinion. **W.W. Freehling,** *The Road to Disunion: Secessionists at Bay 1776-1854,* (Oxford University Press 1990) provides anaysis of the main events of the period.

5 Politics: 1854-61

W.E. Gienapp, *The Origins of the Republican Party,* (Oxford University Press 1987) provides the most detailed account of the birth of the new party. **T.G. Anbinder,** *Nativism and Slavery: The Northern Know Nothings and the Politics of the 1850s,* (Oxford University Press 1992) is the best account of the Know Nothing movement and makes a strong case for the primacy of the slavery issue in Northern politics. **E. Foner,** *Free Soil, Free labor, Free Men: The Ideology of the Republican Party before the Civil War,* (Oxford University Press 1970) remains a key text. As does: **M.F. Holt,** *The Political Crisis of the 1850s,* (Norton 1978) which stresses that the political upheaval of the 1850s owed as much to nativism as to anti-Nebraska sentiment. **K.M. Stampp,** *America in 1857,* (Oxford University Press 1990) is a readable 'snapshot' of what was in Stampp's view a momentous year. **E.B. Smith,** *The Presidency of James Buchanan,* (University Press of Kansas 1975) is one of the few books dealing specifically with Buchanan's presidency. **D.E Fehrenbacher,** *The Dred Scott Case: Its Significance in American Law and Politics,* (Oxford University Press 1978) is actually a history of the slavery expansion issue in American politics. **J.H. Silbey,** T*he American Political Nation 1838-1893,* (Stanford University Press 1991) is worth consulting. P. Finkelman, *His Soul Goes Marching on: Responses to John Brown and the Harper's Ferry Raid,* (University Press of Virginia 1995) looks at the atmosphere post- 1859. **K.M. Stampp,** *And the War Came: The North and the Secession Crisis 1860-1861,* (University of Chicago Press 1964) is still reliable. **W.C. Davis,** *'A Government of Our Own': The Making of the Confederacy,* (Macmillan 1994) is a fascinating account of the men who made the Confederacy.

6 Biographies

One of the best ways to get a deeper understanding of actions and ideas is through biography. Fortunately a large number of first-rate biographies exist of many of the leading figures involved in the events leading to the outbreak of Civil War. These include: **D.H. Donald,** *Lincoln* **(Jonathan Cape 1995); D.E. Fehrenbacher,** *Prelude to Greatness: Lincoln in the 1850s* (McGraw-Hill 1962). **S.B. Oates,** *With*

Malice Toward None: The Life of Abraham Lincoln, (Mentor 1977). **S.B. Oates,** *To Purge This Land with Blood,* (University of Massachusetts Press 1970) an excellent portrait of John Brown. **M. Peterson,** *The Great Triumvirate: Webster, Clay and Calhoun,* (Oxford University Press 1988) is a useful collective biography.

7 Primary Material

Many collections/volumes of primary material are available. Among the most useful are: **H.S. Commager** (ed), *Documents of American History I,* (1963). **K.M. Stampp** (ed), *The Causes of the Civil War,* (Simon and Schuster 1959). **H.S. Commager** (ed), *The Era of Reform 1830-1860,* (Robert Krieger 1960). **F.L. Olmsted,** *The Cotton Kingdom,* edited by A.M. Schlesinger, (Knopf 1966).

More Specialist Works

Students who wish to track down more specialist works can most effectively start via the bibliographies in **J.M. McPherson's** (1988) volume and **D.M. Potter's** (1976) volume.

Index